MASS VIOLENCE IN AMERICA

MASS VIOLENCE IN AMERICA

THE COMPLETE REPORT OF MAYOR LaGUARDIA'S COMMISSION ON THE HARLEM RIOT OF MARCH 19, 1935

ARNO PRESS & THE NEW YORK TIMES

New York • 1969

*

Library of Congress Catalog Card No. 76-90204

*

Reprinted from a manuscript prepared for the
Bureau of Applied Social Research, Columbia University

*

Manufactured in the United States of America

Editorial Note

NATIONS, LIKE MEN, ARE SOMETIMES INTERESTED IN BURYING THE PAST.

In early 1968, after more than five years marked by political assassinations, racial uprisings, campus disorders, mass demonstrations and the violent suppression of protest, *The New York Times Magazine* asked a group of distinguished scholars to reply to the question, "Is America by nature a violent society?" In answer, University of Chicago anthropologist Clifford Geertz wrote:

> "We do not know very well what kind of society we live in, what kind of history we have had, what kind of people we are. We are just now beginning to find out, the hard way . . ."

The proposition was astonishing but correct: what was least understood about domestic political violence was its role in American history. It was common knowledge that the United States had had a Revolution, a Civil War, some trouble with the Indians and a period of labor-management conflict. But one could search the shelves of the nation's great libraries without discovering more than a handful of works on the subject of violence in American history, and these hopelessly out of date.

Historians had generally ignored or soft-pedaled the history of farmer uprisings, native vigilantism, labor-management struggles, ethnic conflicts and race riots; comparative work in the history of social conflict was particularly weak. Sociologists and political scientists in the grip of "consensus" theory tended to treat episodes of mass violence in America as insignificant or aberrational—temporary exceptions to the norm of peaceful progress. Psychologists and behavioral scientists discussed "mob violence" in terms which suggested that riots, revolts, insurrections and official violence were the products of individual or group pathology. All such interpretations had the effect not only of minimizing group violence in America, but of depriving it of political content—hence, of relevance to the present.

As a result, as late as 1968, the rich, multifarious and often terrifying history of domestic political violence was still largely *terra incognita.* So long as most Americans wished to keep certain skeletons locked away in their closets, few scholars would attempt to open doors. Conversely, once the American people, frightened yet emboldened by the sudden reappearance of intense social conflict, began to ask new questions about the past, so did the scholars.

Our purpose in helping Arno Press and *The New York Times* select and publish significant documents in the history of political violence has not been to compound past errors by overemphasizing the role of conflict in American history. On the contrary, our aim has been to provide materials which will aid in the search for an accurate perspective on the present MASS VIOLENCE IN AMERICA includes eyewitness reports, government documents and other descriptive and analytic material relating to mass political violence in the United States. These documents not only provide information—they give the "feel" or "flavor" of past eras of civil disorder by evoking the emotional and political context in which revolts took place. Most of them have long been out of print and are obtainable, if at all, only in the nation's largest libraries.

The scope of this series is wide, ranging from accounts of Indian warfare to descriptions of labor-management violence, from narratives of colonial insurrections to reports on modern racial uprisings. It is not, however, limitless, nor were the constituent volumes carelessly selected. The principle of coherence which guided the selections is implicit in the phrase "mass political violence." "Mass" denotes activity engaged in by large groups rather than individuals acting alone; "political" suggests a relationship between such activity and competition among domestic groups for power, property and prestige; and "violence" is narrowly construed as resulting in physical damage to persons or property. In short, the materials reproduced herein are intended to illuminate the resort to violence by American groups seeking to change or to preserve the status quo. Although historical, they are of interest to any who wishes to understand the causes, nature and direction of domestic political violence, whether they be social scientists, historians or just interested Americans.

Of course, we are particularly hopeful that these volumes will prove useful to those now engaged in curriculum-revision and the teaching of high school and college courses in the area of American studies. What Christopher Jencks and David Reisman term "the Academic Revolution" has made difficult demands on all educators, not the least of which is the demand for courses which are both relevant to the condition of modern America and of the highest academic quality. These volumes are meant to provide raw material for such courses—primary source matter which will help both instructors and students to deepen and enrich their views of the American experience.

Most important, the editors and publisher recognize that these volumes appear during a national crisis which is also a crisis of the spirit, a time in which the public response to various manifestations of civil disorder is increasingly governed by anger, fear and hysteria. In such an atmosphere it is important to recognize that one is not alone in time—that such events have taken place before in America and, unless fundamental changes in our social and political life take place, will probably recur in the future. Our fondest hope is that this work, and others like it, will help to keep alive, in a time of growing unreason, the spirit of reasoned inquiry.

RICHARD E. RUBENSTEIN
The Adlai Stevenson Institute
Chicago, Illinois

ROBERT M. FOGELSON
Harvard-MIT Joint Center for Urban Studies
Cambridge, Massachusetts

THE HARLEM RIOT OF 1935

THE COMPLETE REPORT OF

MAYOR LaGUARDIA'S COMMISSION

ON THE HARLEM RIOT

OF MARCH 19, 1935

FOREWORD

This complete report on the Harlem Riot of 1935 was typed from an account that appeared in the July 18, 1936 edition of the New York Amsterdam News, a Negro weekly. A xeroxed copy of the original Amsterdam News account can be found in Columbia University's Butler Library.

Since it was felt that this report by Mayor LaGuardia's riot commission (which was never officially released to the public) should be more accessible to researchers and other interested persons, the tedious task of typing the report from the xeroxed version was undertaken by our project. This laborious enterprise was completely executed by our incomparable secretary, Sharon Thompson, at Columbia University's Bureau of Applied Social Research. We are deeply grateful to Mrs. Thompson for faithfully recording the words of this historic document with such proficiency--in such a short period of time.

It is important to note, however, that many typographical errors and statistical inaccuracies appear throughout this report. Wherever possible, Mrs. Thompson tried to correct them. But it was not possible to correct most of these errors since we lacked the proper information. Consequently, these inaccuracies are not the fault of our secretary, but are only a faithful reproduction of what appeared in the published account of the Amsterdam News on July 18, 1936.

Of course, none of this would have been possible had not the Amsterdam News the foresight to preserve this important document for posterity. Thus we all are deeply indebted to this newspaper for its enterprising efforts.

Dr. Robert M. Fogelson, Principal Investigator
Associate Professor of History and Urban Planning
Massachusetts Institute of Technology

Dr. Robert B. Hill, Project Director
Research Associate
Bureau of Applied Social Research
Columbia University

January, 1969

TABLE OF CONTENTS

Introduction	SUMMARY BY NEW YORK AMSTERDAM NEWS	1
Chapter 1	EVENTS OF MARCH 19 (1935)	7
Chapter 2	THE PUBLIC HEARINGS	19
Chapter 3	THE NEGRO COMMUNITY IN HARLEM	27
Chapter 4	THE RELIEF SITUATION	44
Chapter 5	THE HOUSING PROBLEM	63
Chapter 6	THE PROBLEM OF EDUCATION AND RECREATION . .	77
Chapter 7	HEALTH AND HOSPITALIZATION	92
Chapter 8	CRIME AND THE POLICE	106
Chapter 9	CONCLUSIONS AND RECOMMENDATIONS	122
Appendix	CAPTIONS OF PHOTOGRAPHS	136

THE NEW YORK AMSTERDAM NEWS
July 18, 1936

COMPLETE RIOT REPORT BARED

REPORT MAYOR HID COMPLETE IN THIS ISSUE
Amsterdam News Is First to Publish Harlem Study

Answering the public's demand to get the word-by-word report of the Mayor's Commission which investigated conditions in Harlem following the March, 1935, rioting, the Amsterdam News, in this issue, puts into print every word of this report which Mayor F.H. LaGuardia has insistently refused to release, although His Honor has had it in his possession since March 19, 1936.

From time to time, segments of this 35,000-word document have reached the public, but this is the very first time that anyone, outside the commission itself, and the Mayor, has been able to read the report.

More than the complete report, the Amsterdam News is here making public for the first time the original chapter of conclusions--Chapter IX--which was considered too hot, too caustic, too critical, too unfavorable by the Mayor, and was allegedly revamped by the commission to make it more to his liking. The Chapter Nine in the official report in the Mayor's hands is the softer, less biting chapter.

Chapter Included

Word for word, paragraph by paragraph, some of the findings of the Commission will be found to be nothing new--no facts that Harlemites and New Yorkers have not known, or could not have known long before the riots of March 19.

Here, however, these conditions are reviewed and uttered by a commission having the sanction of the head of the City government, and conclusions are made, not only by the social workers and reformers, but by the "salt of the earth," the man in the street, the men and women who feel most the rigors of starvation, the spiked heels of the police, and the crushing load of high rents and discrimination in employment most.

Reviews Events

The Commission, headed by Dr. Charles H. Roberts, 233 West 139th Street, and consisting of both whites and Negroes, lawyers, preachers, civic and public servants, reviewed the occurrences of the March afternoon, when a teenage boy, Lino Rivera, stole a pocket knife from a 125th Street five and ten cent store. It tells again of the combination of circumstances which made people to believe the young Negro boy had been beaten to death, and of how the police, first, inefficiently, and next, ruthlessly, tried to meet the excitement of the people.

The report tells how the commission could not locate a "committee of women shoppers" which the police said it had allowed to go into the basement of the store to verify that the boy had not been killed, and infers that no such committee of shoppers ever existed.

Negroes Chased Away

It records how the police told inquiring Negroes that the Rivera affair was none of their business, and how honest, decent citizens were chased away both from the store and the nearby police station when they tried to get the truth.

On the question of the crowd-inciting leaflets issued by the Young Liberators and which were supposed to play a prominent part in fanning the riot flames, the Commission notes that the leaflets did not hit the streets until 7:30 P.M., and, therefore, the group "were not responsible for the disorders and attacks on property which were already in full swing. Already a tabloid in screaming headlines was telling the city that a race riot was going on in Harlem," the report states.

Communist Angle Touched

Speaking on the part the Communists played in the rioting, the Commission declares:

> "While one, in view of the available facts, would hesitate to give Communists full credit for preventing the outbreak from becoming a race riot, they deserve more credit than any other element in Harlem for preventing a physical conflict between whites and Negroes."

Long felt hostility to the police, resentment at the inability to get economic opportunities in the midst of plenty, were some of the reasons for the rioting, the report states, and then detailedly it records its findings under sections entitled:

"How Negro Harlem Makes a Living,"
"The Relief Situation,"
"Housing Problem,"
"Education and Recreation,"
"Crime and Police."

Relief Problems Told

It reports that Negroes, who long felt that they could not get adequate and sympathetic assistance from welfare agencies found no improvement of conditions when the city home relief bureaus were established.

Then into 110 typewritten pages, the document continues, ending with its "Conclusion and Recommendations." Here the original sentiment of the commission is given; later this chapter was given a veneer to please the Mayor.

The nearness of the relief situation to the rank and file of the people was shown at the public hearings held at the Seventh District Municipal Courthouse, 447 West 151st Street. These were the most hectic meetings, the spectators crowded the place, they demanded to be heard, they booed and heckled home relief functionaries. They frightened city and commission, and in the end, the commission had to call off the open hearings.

Raps Police Army

"Today, extra police stand guard on the corners and mounted patrolmen ride through the streets of Harlem," the closing chapter says after briefly reviewing the cause of the rioting.

"To the citizens of Harlem," it continues, "they (the police) symbolize the answer of the city authorities to their protest of March 19. To Harlem this show of force simply signifies that property will be protected at any cost; but it offers no assurance that the legitimate demands of the citizens of the community for work and decent living conditions will be heeded.

"Hence, this show of force only tends to make the conditions which were responsible for the occurrence last March 19 more irritating. And so long as these conditions persist, no one knows when they will lead to recurrence, with possibly greater violence, of the happenings of that night."

Then the Commission goes down the list of its recommendations.

It makes recommendations seeking to prevent the present broadguaged discrimination against Negroes in employment.

It suggests immediate improvements in relief administration, and future adjustments concerning relief policy.

It makes recommendations on education and recreation, specifically asking for new school buildings.

It asks that colored doctors be admitted to all city hospitals, that

Harlem Hospital be given a cleaning out.

It requests for a citizens' committee to hear citizens' complaints against the police.

Mayor Tries to Reply

Some of these recommendations the Mayor has attempted to answer at recent public meetings, mostly by saying that he has already done the things the commission asked to be done. But the Mayor has never made public the report, and his police commissioner has openly stated that he will keep his armed police army in Harlem, and if he had more men to spare, he would send them up here.

Following the Chicago riots of 1920, when Dr. Charles S. Johnson wrote the report of the Chicago Commission, the report was published by the University of Chicago Press and has since become a very important reference work used all over the country by government bodies and universities.

Professor Directed Studies

Dr. E. Franklin Frazier, professor of sociology at Howard University, was engaged as director of the studies and surveys on which the commission based its report. Different members of the commission headed sub-committees, and presided over the public hearings.

Early in the public hearings. one of its members put himself on record as believing Communists responsible for the rioting, and later disagreed with the temporary report made on police brutality. The dissenting member is the Rev. Father William R. McCann, pastor of St. Charles Borromeo Roman Catholic Church, West 141st Street.

The Amsterdam News does not believe that Father McCann signed the final report, as it does not have the formal, routine letter submitting the document to Mayor LaGuardia.

Committee Citywide

The original membership of the committee included Dr. Charles Roberts, chairman; Oswald Garrison Villard, white liberal publisher, vice-chairman; Mrs. Eunice Hunton Carter, secretary; Hubert Delany, Tax Commissioner; Countee Cullen, poet; A. Philip Randolph, President of the Brotherhood of Sleeping Car Porters; Municipal Judge Charles E. Toney.

The white members of the committee included William Jay Schieffelin, trustee of Tuskegee Institute; Morris Ernst and Arthur Garfield Hayes, prominent attorneys; Col. John J. Grimley of the 369th Infantry, and Father McCann.

CHAPTER I

Events of March 19

At about 2:30 on the afternoon of March 19, 1935, Lino Rivera, a 16-year-old colored boy, stole a knife from a counter in the rear of E.H. Kress and Company on 125th street. He was seen by the manager of the store, Jackson Smith, and an assistant, Charles Hurley, who were on the balcony at the time. Mr. Hurley and another employee overtook the boy before he was able to make his escape through the front door. When the two men took the knife from Rivera's pocket and threatened him with punishment, the boy in his fright tried to cling to a pillar and bit the hands of his captors. Rivera was finally taken to the front entrance, where Mounted Patrolman Donahue was called. The boy was then taken back into the store by the officer, who asked the manager if an arrest was desired. While Mr. Smith, the manager, instructed the officer to let the culprit go free--as he had done in many cases before--an officer from the Crime Prevention Bureau was sent to the store.

This relatively unimportant case of juvenile pilfering would never have acquired the significance which it later took on had not a fortuitous combination of subsequent events made it the spark that set aflame the smouldering resentments of the people of Harlem against racial discrimination and poverty in the midst of plenty. Patrolman Donahue, in order to avoid the curious and excited spectators, took the boy through the basement to the rear entrance on 124th Street. But his act only confirmed the outcry of a hysterical Negro woman that they had taken "the boy to the basement to beat him up." Likewise, the appearance of the ambulance which had been summoned to dress the wounded hands of the boy's captors not only seemed to substantiate her charge, but, when it left empty, gave color to another rumor that the boy was dead. By an odd trick of fate, still another incident furnished the final confirmation of the rumor of the boy's death to the excited throng of shoppers. A hearse which was usually kept in a garage opposite the store on 124th street was parked in front of the store entrance while the driver entered the store to see his brother-in-law. The rumor of the death of the boy, which became now to the aroused Negro shoppers an established fact, awakened the deep-seated sense of wrongs and denials and even memories of injustices in the South. One woman was heard to cry out that the treatment was "just like down South where they lynch us." The deep sense of wrong expressed in this remark was echoed in the rising resentment which turned the hundred or more shoppers into an indignant crowd.

Policeman's Attitude Arouses Crowd

The sporadic attempts on the part of the police to assure the crowd within the store that no harm had been done the boy fell upon unbelieving ears, partly because no systematic attempt was made to let representatives of the crowd determine the truth for themselves, and partly because of the attitude of the policeman. According to the testimony of one policeman, a committee of women from among the shoppers was permitted to search the basement, but these women have never been located. On the other hand, when the crowd became too insistent about learning the fate of the boy, the police told them that it was none of their business and attempted to shove them towards the door. This only tended to infuriate the crowd and was interpreted by them as further evidence of the suppression of a wronged race. At 5:30 it became necessary to close the store.

The closing of the store did not stay the rumors that were current inside. With incredible swiftness the feelings and attitude of the outraged crowd of shoppers was communicated to those on 125th street and soon all of Harlem was repeating the rumor that a Negro boy had been murdered in the basement of Kress' store. The first sign of the reaction of the community appeared when a group of men attempted to start a public meeting at a nearby corner. When the police ordered the group to move from the corner, they set up a stand in front of Kress' store. A Negro who acted as chairman introduced a white speaker. Scarcely had the speaker uttered the first words of his address to the crowd when someone threw a missile through the window of Kress' store. This was the signal for the police to drag the speaker from the stand and disperse the crowd. Immediately, the crowd reassembled across the street and another speaker attempted to address the crowd from a porch on a lamppost. He was pulled down from his post and arrested along with the other speaker on a charge of "unlawful assemblage." These actions on the part of the police only tended to arouse resentment in the crowd which was increasing all the time along 125th Street. From 125th street the crowds spread to Seventh Avenue and Lenox Avenue and the smashing of windows and looting of shops gathered momentum as the evening and the night came on.

Liberator's Leaflet Discussed

During the late afternoon the rumor that a Negro boy had been beaten and killed in Kress' store reached the headquarters of a group comprised mainly of Negroes and known as the "Young Liberators." The purpose of this organization is the protection of the rights of Negroes. Although it is not a Communist group, as has been rumored, it has Communists among its members, one being a member of its executive committee. According to Joseph Taylor, the president of the organization, upon hearing the story of the death of the Negro boy, he went to Kress' store in order to verify the rumor and when he was refused entrance to the store he went to the nearby police station from which he was also ordered away. Accepting the rumor as true (although Mr.

Taylor denies that he was personally responsible) the Young Liberators printed and circulated an exciting leaflet.

CHILD BRUTALLY BEATEN!

WOMAN ATTACKED BY BOSS AND COPS.

CHILD NEAR DEATH.

One hour ago a 12-year-old Negro boy was brutally beaten by the management of Kress' Five and Ten Cent Store.

The boy is near death, mercilessly beaten because they thought he had stolen a five-cent knife. A Negro woman, who sprang to the defense of the boy, had her arm broken by the thug and was then arrested.

WORKERS! NEGRO AND WHITE.

Protest against this Lynch Attack of Innocent Negro People.

Demand Release of Boy and Woman.

Demand the immediate arrest of the management responsible for this lynch attack.

Don't Buy at Kress'.

Stop Police Brutality in Negro Harlem.

JOIN THE PICKET LINE.

About the same time, the Young Communist League, without attempting to verify the rumor, issued a similar leaflet. Since neither of these leaflets, according to the testimony given to the commission, appeared on the streets before 7:30 p.m., the actions of these two groups, though exhibiting a lack of due regard for the possible serious consequences of acting on mere rumors, were not responsible for the disorder and attacks on property which were already in full swing. Already a tabloid in screaming headlines was telling the city that race riot was going on in Harlem.

In fact, the Communists defend their part in the riot on the grounds that they prevented the riot from becoming a clash between whites and Negroes. While one, in view of the available facts, would hesitate to give the Communists full credit for preventing the outbreak from becoming a race riot, they deserve more credit than any other element in Harlem for preventing a physical conflict between whites and blacks. The young white men who mounted the ladder and lamp post on 125th street and were beaten and arrested because they took the parts of the indignant Negro crowds certainly changed the complexion of the outbreak. It was probably due in some measure to the activities of these racial leaders, both white and black, that the crowds attacked property rather than persons.

Communists Not Cause of Riot

In fact, the distinguishing feature of this outbreak was that it was an attack upon property and not upon persons. In the beginning, to be sure, the resentment was expressed against whites--but whites who owned stores and who, while exploiting Negroes, denied them an opportunity to work. Although the Jewish merchants in the Harlem community naturally came in for their share of the attacks upon the stores, there does not seem to be any foundation for the report circulated at first that these attacks were directed mainly at them. While, of course, tiny motives were responsible for the actions of these crowds, it seems that as they grew more numerous and more active, the personality or racial identity of the owners of the stores faded out and the property itself became the object of their fury. Stores owned by Negroes were not always spared if they happened to be in the path of those roving crowds, bent upon the destruction and the confiscation of property.

Outbreak Seen As Spontaneous

From its inception, as we have pointed out, the outbreak was a spontaneous and unpremediated action on the part, first, of women shoppers in Kress' store and, later, of the crowds on 125th street that had been formed as the result of the rumor of a boy's death in the store. As the fever of excitement based upon this rumor spread to other sections of the community, other crowds, formed by many unemployed standing about the streets and other onlookers, sprang up spontaneously. At no time does it seem that these crowds were under the direction of any single individual or that they acted as a part of a conspiracy against law and order. The very susceptibility which the people in the community showed towards this rumor--which was more or less vague, depending upon the circumstances under which it was communicated--was due to the feeling of insecurity produced by years of unemployment and deep-seated resentment against the many forms of discrimination which they had suffered as a racial minority.

While it is difficult to estimate the actual number of persons who participated in the outburst, it does not seem, from available sources of information, that more than a few thousand were involved. These were not concentrated at any time in one place. Crowds formed here and there as the rumors spread. When a crowd was dispersed by the police, it often re-formed again. These crowds constantly changed their make-up. When bricks thrown through store windows brought the police, the crowds would often dissolve, only to gather again and continue their assaults upon property. Looting often followed the smashing of store windows. The screaming of sirens, the sound of pistol shots and the cracking of glass created in many a need for destruction and excitement. Rubbish, flower pots, or any object at hand were tossed from windows into the street. People seized property when there was no possible use which it would serve. They acted as if there were a chance to seize what rightfully belonged to them but had long been withheld. The crowds showed various needs and changed their mood from time to time. (Some of the destruction was carried on in a playful spirit. Even the looting, which has furnished many an amuseing tale, was sometimes done in the spirit of children taking preserves from a closet to which they have accidentally found the key.) The mood of these crowds was determined in many cases by the attitude of the police towards their unruly conduct. But, in the end, neither the threats nor the reassurances of the police could restrain these spontaneous out bursts until the crowds had spent themselves in giving release to their pent-up emotions. The final dramatic attempt on the part of the police to placate the populace by having the unharmed Lino Rivera photographed with the Negro police lieutenant, Samuel Battle, only furnished the basis for the rumor that Rivera, who was on probation for having placed a slug in a subway turnstile, was being used as a substitute to deceive the people.

Hostility to Police Many Years Old

Lack of confidence in the police and even hostility towards these representatives of the law were evident at every stage of the riot. This attitude of the people of Harlem has been built up over many years of experience with the police in this section. During the early stages of the excitement in the store when there was still time for the police to prevent the spread of the rumor, they assumed, according to reliable witnesses, the attitude which is reputed to be their general attitude towards the citizens of the Harlem community. One witness described the scene in the store around 4:30 or 5 o'clock in the afternoon as follows:

"There were just a few policemen. They walked through the store to the back. Then something happened in the back. Some people say a woman screamed. All of the group surged to the back of the store. When I got back there, they were driven forward by the policeman who was in front of them, and one woman particularly demanded that they produce the manager, and the boy and the policeman told her it was none of her damned business. All of this time I heard no explanation, nothing except among the people themselves indignation grew higher. In the meantime more policemen came into the store and they said, 'drive these people out,' and became rather rough and pushed the people. Finally they had a few women out of the store. I said to the policeman, 'can't you tell us what happened?' He said, 'If you know what's good for you, you better get on home.'"

Although Patrolman Timothy Shannon testified that he appointed a committee of three women to go to the basement of the store to see that no boy was there, he felt that a more effective procedure; namely, to have shown the unharmed boy to the crowd "was up to my superiors." Here was the notion of the police towards those who attempted to hold a street meeting more assuring when they broke up the meeting before anyone had spoken a word. Even if the police excuse such action on the grounds that they were acting in an emergency did not require them to take two of the speakers to jail, beat them up, leave them without food for almost twenty-four hours, and refuse to permit them to get in touch with their attorneys. Moreover, the extreme barbarity which was shown towards at least one of these speakers was seemingly motivated by the fact that these policemen who made degregatory and threatening remarks concerning Negroes were outraged because white men dared to take the part of Negroes.

All Police Not Found Tactless

At the same time, it should be said in fairness to the police that many of them handled the situation with tact and understanding and even in their attempts to restrain the crowds showed neither animous nor brutality. It is needless to say that in a trying situation like that of March 19, it was difficult at times for a policeman to carry out orders to protect property and restrain lawless conduct and at the same time show a humane regard for human life. Yet, after we have made allowances for all the difficulties involved in such a situation, the shooting of Lloyd Hobbs, a sixteen-year-old boy, on the night of the riot, was inexcusable and brutal on the part of the police. This was the one outstanding tragic event of the entire disorder.

Two high school boys, Lloyd and Russell Hobbs, brothers, on their way home from a motion picture house at 12:45 a.m. were attracted by a crowd in front of Greenberg's automobile accessory shop on Seventh Avenue near 128th street. They were standing there, according to the statement of Russell Hobbs and several witnesses, when a police car containing two policemen, one of whom was Patrolman John Heineray, drove up. When Heineray alighted with a revolver in his hand, the crowd, including the Hobbs brothers, began to run. Lloyd, instead of running northward with the crowd, turned left at 129th street and crossed the street diagonally. As he reached the further sidewalk, Heineray fired, the bullet passing through the boy's body and into his right hand. According to the testimony of several witnesses, the police fired without calling upon the boy to halt and struck him with his first and only shot. Lloyd Hobbs was taken to the Harlem Hospital, where he died a few days later.

Discuss Shooting of Lloyd Hobbs

Heineray claimed that when the police car reached 129th street, he and his partner heard a window of the store crash and that during the time they came to a halt before the store, a distance of 175 feet from where they were when they heard the crash. Lloyd Hobbs had climed into the window, passed some of the loot out to members of the crowd, and was in the act of jumping out. Moreover, Heineray claimed that he ordered Lloyd to halt and that, when the boy continued to run with part of the loot in his hand, he fired the fatal shot.

Besides the testimony of witnesses, there are several facts which cast serious doubts on the statement of the police. Certain automobile accessories consisting of a wrench and part of a horn, which the boy was supposed to have dropped during his flight, were not turned over to the police department until eight days after the shooting. They were produced by Heineray and were seen for the first time by Detective O'Brien, who was investigating the casein the office of the district attorney on April 1. Moreover, the original record of the arrest of Lloyd Hobbs made no mention of goods having been found. The police record was subsequently altered and a statement concerning the loot was deftly inserted.

The shooting of Lloyd Hobbs, a boy having a good record both in school and in the community, and being a member of a family of good standing and character, has left the impression upon the community that the life of a Negro is of little value in the eyes of the police. The circumstances surrounding this case exclude the excuse that the policeman was dealing with a dangerous criminal who threatened the safety and welfare of the community. In fact, it seems that many of the Negroes beaten and arrested on the night of the riot did not offer as great a threat to security of life and property as the alleged act of pilfering with which Hobbs was charged. It has been reported that only the hoodlum element and criminal class participated in the looting of stores.

While it seems indisputable that the criminal element took advantage of the disorders, it seems equally true from the testimony of observers that many youngsters who could not be classed as criminals joined the looting crowds in a spirit of pure adventure. Even some grown-up men and women who had probably never committed a criminal act before, but had suffered years of privation, seized the opportunity to express their resentment against discrimination in employment and the exclusive rights of property.

"Respectable" Not Among Rioters

Of course, the respectable and secure members of the community refrained from joining the crowds, and on the next morning some of them wanted to issue a statement to the effect that they condemned the actions of the mobs. But this was not the temper or attitude of all the respectable and law-abiding members of the community. Among all classes there was a feeling that the outburst of the populace was justified and that it represented a protest against discrimination and privations resulting from unemployment. While they readily acknowledged that they would not use such violent means to register their protests, they were nevertheless in sympathy with those who had done so. As one professional man, who has known discrimination and felt the pinch of the economic crisis through the unemployment of his clientele, remarked: "These poor, ignorant and rough Negroes on 125th street were fighting my battle." Such frank statements made in private bespeak more authentically the general mood and temper of the community than volumes of formal public statements by leaders.

What, then, was the deeper significance of the events of March 19? Why should the mere detention of a boy for pilfering a knife have become the signal for a general alarm throughout the Harlem community? Why was the community so susceptible to an unfounded rumor which many continue to believe in spite of the sworn testimony of reliable witnesses? Why did large masses spring up spontaneously all over the community and spend their fury in the demolition of property? These are some of the questions which this report proposes to answer.

The explosion on March 19 would never have been set off by the trifling incident described above had not exciting economic and social forces created a state of emotional tension which sought release upon the slightest provocation. As long as the economic and social forces which were responsible for that condition to operate, a state of tension will exist in Harlem and recurrent outbursts may occur. Before attempting to answer the questions raised by the riot, let us pause to view the public hearings where the community was given a chance to air its grievances and present its demands before the representatives of the constituted authorities who govern Harlem.

CHAPTER II

The Public Hearings

The commission appointed by Mayor LaGuardia to inquire into the conditions which caused the outbreak on March 19 divided its work among six subcommittees. Each committee was charged with the investigation of a special phase of community life, either because it had long been a source of irritation or appeared to the public mind as a form of injustice towards the citizens of Harlem. For example, the Committee on Crime and the Police took as its task not only the investigation of the riot but also an investigation of the general behavior and attitude of the police in the community.

Since the people of Harlem had suffered especially because of the depression and had become acutely sensitive to discriminatory practices towards Negroes in regard to jobs, another committee, the Committee on Discrimination in Employment undertook the investigation of discrimination against Negroes in regard to employment. Likewise, as the relief situation in Harlem had created much unrest and criticism from the time of its inception, a committee on home relief was appointed to inquire into this phase of the problem. Naturally, Harlem Hospital, which had been a storm center and subject of agitation for over a decade, could not escapt the scrutiny of the commission which delegated to the Committee on Hospitals the duty of investigating the problem of Negro health and hospitalization in the community. In an investigation of the kind undertaken by the commission, it was impossible to overlook the school situation which had been a source of periodical complaints. Therefore, a committee on education was set up to seek reliable information on this phase of the institutional life of the community. Last, but not by any means least important, the housing of the Negro was made the subject of investigation by the committee on housing.

Six Committees Conducted Hearings

These six committees, beginning on March 30 with a hearing on the riot, conducted twenty-one public and four closed hearings in the Seventh District Municipal Building on 131st street. They invited to appear at these hearings persons representing all strata of the population of Harlem as well as officials of institutions and representatives of agencies interested in the community. Anyone who had a complaint against any public official or a laborer in the most menial occupation was given the same opportunity to express himself before any one of these committees as the most powerful representative of private or public interests. While the response to the invitations of the various committees was on the whole, as the numbers indicate, favorable, employers in key positions in industry, important officials in the public utilities and in the labor unions refused to appear or gave flimsy excuses for not appearing before the hearings. The witnesses who did appear represented either those who were interested in the welfare of the community or those who had felt the effects of discrimination and frustration in their legitimate aspirations or had suffered from poverty and unemployment.

Some idea of the extent to which the community grasped the opportunity offered by the commission to express itself is gleamed from the number of witnesses who testified voluntarily at these hearings. A hundred and sixty witnesses took the stand during the two and one-half months in which hearings were held and gave testimony on the various problems facing the Negro in Harlem. Many of these witnesses appeared several times and submitted not only to questioning by the commission but also to cross-examination by experienced lawyers and none-too-sympathetic members of the audiences.

The audiences varied, according to the publicity given the hearings and the opportunity for attendance from slightly less than a score to more than five hundred. At least a hundred and twenty-two persons in the audiences who cross-examined these witnesses, gave their names and are identifiable. They, as in the case of the witnesses, represented every section and interest in the community.

Public at Hearings Far From Passive

However, these figures fail to give any idea of the temper and attitude of the audiences which attended the hearings. From the street, it became clear that the various committees, especially those holding hearings on subjects which were the primary cause of unrest in Harlem, were not to listen to testimony before a passive public. The commission as well as the witness found themselves face to face with an aroused public which demanded that its grievances should be heard and that no technicalities of court procedure or rules of order were to thwart its right to be heard. Naturally, it was difficult at times to conduct orderly public hearings and at the same time to permit the justified expression of popular resentment against existing conditions.

Nevertheless, it seemed to the commission that the wiser course was not to insist upon the strict decorum of court procedure and thereby exclude the participation of the public, but to allow, as far as it was consistent with the purposes of the hearings, the public as represented by these audiences to subject the statement of witnesses and the conduct of the commission to the closest scrutiny. Although, on one occasion, at the last public hearing of the commission, conducted by the committee on relief, it was necessary to adjourn the hearing because a court officer attempted to enforce silence on a member of the audience and thereby created a popular outburst, the policy pursued by the commission was justified by the results obtained. The few closed hearings conducted by the commission were held only in order to afford protection to teachers who were unwilling to expose themselves to possible reprisals and to give an official of a social agency an opportunity to present a defense of his position in an unprejudiced atmosphere.

Closed Hearings Very Few

The temper of the public and its skeptical attitude became evident when the first hearing was held on the events of March 19. It was insinuated by witnesses and charged by members of the audience that Lino Rivera was not the boy involved in the initial disturbance in Kress' store. But such charge and insinuations remained in the realm of rumors for no witness was produced who gave a description of any other boy, nor was any evidence submitted to show that any other boy in Harlem had been beaten or was missing. On the other hand, in addition to the statements of Rivera himself and employees of the store and the police, the indisputable testimony of Mr. L. F. Coiss, a respected citizen of Harlem, who was in the store, that Rivera was the boy, left no doubt concerning the boy's identity in the minds of the members of the commission. The persistence of the belief in this rumor in the face of reliable testimony to the contrary was indicative of the skeptical mood of the people in the audience who openly expressed a lack of confidence in the police and the representatives of established authority. In fact, at times lack of confidence in the impartiality and sincerity of the commission was expressed by members of the various audiences who were always alert to the slightest suggestion of an attempt to control the free expression of opinion.

The pent-up resentment of the people against discrimination and injustices expressed itself most forcibly in regard to the police and relief situation in Harlem: first, in their minds was the brutal killing of Lloyd Hobbs, which stood out as a symbol of the constant threat that the police had offered to their peace, security and very existence. As testimony was given from time to time by reliable witnesses of infringements upon the personal rights and of the brutality practiced by the police, it was often difficult to restrain the vociferous condemnations of the people in the audience. The somewhat similar attitude of the audience towards the question of home relief revealed that a long period of unemployment and enforced poverty had created an emotional tension that would be a threat to the order of the community as long as the situation continued.

Emotional Tension Held Threat to Order

The question naturally arises: To what extent did the people who comprised the audiences at the public hearings represent the great mass of the people of Harlem? Isn't it possible, if not probable, that the people who gathered at these hearings represented a small minority of disgruntled and unadjusted persons in the community? Or were they not professional agitators or the spokesmen of propaganda organizations? Undoubtedly, not only did the unadjusted and the disgruntled take advantage of the occasion to air their discontent, but all sorts of propaganda organizations, some probably never heard of before in Harlem, used the opportunity to give publicity to their aims and to make converts to their philosophies. The charge has been brought against the Communists especially that they attempted to "steal the show" or used the hearings as a platform to promulgate their doctrines.

It was perfectly natural that the Communists should have utilized to the full the opportunity which the public hearings offered to act as the defenders of an expressed minority. Not only did they play this role with consummate skill, and this assertion does not imply any lack of sincerity, but the experienced and shrewd lawyers of the International Labor Defense translated the groping, and often incoherent, queries of the common man into clear, searching questions which prevented equivocation and subterfuge on the part of witnesses. However, it should be mentioned that the testimony on Harlem Hospital, which Mr. James W. Ford had read before the commission was, on the whole, a factual statement supported by statistics. In the final analysis, the main role which the Communists played at the public hearings was by no means that of professional agitators and propagandists; they only defined and gave direction to the often vague dissatisfaction of the people, and attempted to interpret injustices which were regarded merely as racial persecution as a phase of the general expression of the submerged classes. Although it is difficult to say how far they succeeded in accomplishing this end, they certainly played a part in preventing the indignation which was expressed at these hearings from becoming purely the resentment of blacks against whites.

Audiences Found "Truly Cross-Section"

A partial answer at least to the question, to what extent the people who attended the hearings represented the temper and attitude of the entire Harlem community, may be found in the composition of the audiences. A survey of the spectators at the various hearings indicated that all elements in the population were represented. The most secure and respectable, the cultured and educated, were present and followed the hearings with the same interest as the poor and ignorant who were defenseless in the face of discrimination and had suffered most from the debasing effects of poverty. The audiences were truly a cross-section of the Harlem population, and one is justified in concluding that their various reactions at the hearings expressed the general feelings of the community just as the outbreak on March 19 gave expression to the general unrest in the community.

It might with some logic be assumed that in the tense atmosphere surrounding many of these public hearings little reliable information or testimony of value could be adduced, But it would be a mistake to draw conclusion on purely a priori grounds. While it is true that such unrelaible testimony was given and that witnesses were antagonized or perhaps in a few cases intimidated to a slight extent, a wealth of valuable and authentic information was given the commission. In many cases witnesses read from manuscripts or supported their testimony with documents and statistics. During the hearings which lasted in some cases from morning until evening, there were long enough periods of quiet and thoughtful attention on the part of audiences to allow witnesses to give testimony without being influenced either by fear within or interruption from without. At the hearings which attracted smaller audiences because the information presented contained little of the dramatic element, there was no lack of either solemnity or decorum.

The commission in its efforts to secure information concerning the social and economic conditions which had brought about the outburst on March 19 in Harlem did not rely solely upon the testimonies given at its hearings. It engaged a professional sociologist with considerable experiences in the field of social research and placed under his direction a staff of thirty men and women carefully selected from the staff of the Home Relief Bureau. The chapters which follow present the essence of the findings of the director of the study and his staff who carried on investigations over a period of eight months.

CHAPTER III

The Negro Community in Harlem

Negro Community in Harlem

In the Harlem community which, for the purpose of this report, includes the area bounded on the north and south by 181st and Ninety-ninth streets and on the east by the East and Harlem Rivers and on the west by the Hudson River, there are over 200,000 Negroes.* According to a survey by the New York City Housing Authority in 1934, the Negro population in this area comprised 56,157 family groups. While these Negro families represented 31.1 per cent of all the families in the area, the Negro population is concentrated near the center of the area and is surrounded, with the exception of the Puerto Ricans on the south, by whites, about a third of whom are foreign born.

In spite of its poverty and the fact that the majority of its population is from the rural South or the West Indies, the Negro community is not a slum area, but constitutes in many respects a city in itself. In the area between Eighth and Lenox Avenues and 134th and 135th streets there are to be found the same population characteristics, the same types of institutions, and the same manifestations of behavior as distinguished the centers of most modern urban communities.

Here the smallest proportion of children in the Negro population are to be found in conjunction with the largest proportion of single men and women in the community. In this same area we find Negro businesses and places of amusement concentrated, and the greatest amount of mobility represented in the movement of people and the discrimination of race. From this center, which includes the location of the first Negro residents in the area, the Negro community spreads out in all directions.

Population Rise Discussed

The rapid growth of the Negro community in Harlem is recorded in the federal census figures and other sources of information on this area. Between 1910 and 1933 the Negro population grew from 23,000 to 83,807, which represented an increase of 191.3 per cent. During the next decade the rate of increase was 244 per cent, the Negro population being 204,313 in 1930. Since 1930 the Negro population has seemingly become almost stationary for, according to the New York City Housing Authority, there were 204,630 Negroes in this area in 1934. In considering the numerical growth of the Negro population in this area, it should be kept in mind that this population is composed mainly of adults. As far back as 1910 about 72 per cent of the population was twenty years of age or over, and since then, because of migration, the proportion has increased, so that at the present time three-fourths of the population is made up ofpersons twenty or over. In this connection another feature of the population also deserves attention. In the Harlem area the percentage of Negro women in the population exceeds that of men by five per cent.

While these figures show the rapid growth of the Negro population and something of its general character, they give us indication of the social and economic problems that have attended the incursion during the last fifteen years of 120,000 people, representing a different racial group and without experience in urban life into the heart of an already fairly densely populated community.

---

*The 1930 federal census statistics for this area were as follows: Native whites of native parentage, 134,669; native whites of foreign or mixed parentages, 187,725; foreign-born whites, 187,713; Negro, 204,313.

The fact that the sudden expansion of the Negro community has not resulted in any serious friction with other racial groups in the area has tended to obscure the seriousness and extent of the problems of the Negro community. Yet, the Negro in Harlem has been confronted at all times with the problem of securing suitable homes and free access to the institutions which were intended to serve the needs of the community. Although, strange as it might seem, the presence of this large Negro community in Harlem is due primarily to economic forces, particularly the labor demands growing out of the feverish industrial activity during the World War, the problem of primary importance to the Harlem Negro has been that of securing employment.

How Negro Harlem Makes Living

While there are no available statistics on the occupations of Negroes in the Harlem area, we can get a fairly accurate picture of the situation from the census figures for the borough of Manhattan as a whole. From the table below, it appears that Negro men here since 1910 shifted from domestic and personal service to manufacturing and mechanical industries and transportation. While a similar shift is noticeable for Negro women, they have drifted back to domestic and persoanl service. Both men and women, the women more so than the men, have shown gains in professional services and clerical occupations. However, these figures should not be taken at their face value as indications of the upward movement of the Negro in the economic structure. A closer analysis of the figures on occupations show that, while the proportion of Negro men and women in manufacturing and mechanical industries had doubled since 1910, they are still in the lowest-paid and unskilled occupations.

For example, a third of the Negro men in manufacturing and mechanical industries are common laborers and about another third are unskilled workers. The same is true of Negroes classified under transportation, where about a third are working as common laborers and a fourth as stevedores and dock hands. While it is recognized that a large proportion of Negroes who have had little experience in industry and trade would naturally be found in the lowest-paid and unskilled occupations, because of forces inherent in our competitive economic system, yet, as we shall see below, discrimination and non-economic factors are responsible to a large extent for the present state of affairs.

TABLE I.

PERCENTAGE OF NEGRO MEN AND WOMEN EMPLOYED IN MAJOR OCCUPATIONAL DIVISIONS IN THE BOROUGH OF MANHATTAN, NEW YORK CITY, 1910-1930

	1910		1920		1930	
Occupations	Male	Female	Male	Female	Male	Female
Manufacturing and Mechanical Industries	11.8	8.7	23.6	26.6	22.1	17.2
Transportation	16.1	0.1	19.8	1.0	17.5	0.4
Trade	4.5	0.8	6.9	0.7	8.7	1.0
Public Service	1.5	...	2.2	...	1.4	...
Professional Service	8.3	1.8	2.0	2.0	4.3	3.7
Domestic and Personal Service..................	54.1	85.4	40.9	70.1	39.8	76.1
Clerical	4.3	0.8	6.3	1.2	6.1	1.7
Total	96.6	98.7	99.4	99.9	99.9	100.0

The Harlem Negro endeavors to make a living, not only by offering his labor for sale, but also through setting up business enterprises of his own. A survey of 58 of the 78 census tracts in the Harlem area, in which (?) per cent of the total population was Negro, heard that Negroes conduct 1,9__ (?) or 18.6 per cent of the 10,319 businesses. The main type of businesses conducted by Negroes differ considerably from the chief businesses in which whites are engaged. More than a third--38.5 per cent--of the Negro businesses provide personal service, such as barber shops, beauty parlors and cleaning and pressing shops, where little capital is needed. On the other hand, the same percentage--36.3--of the businesses conducted by whites provide the basic needs of the community.

These businesses include grocery stores, meat markets, bakeries, coal and ice companies, restaurants, clothing, department and furniture stores. Only 18.4 of the Negro businesses in the community provide such basic needs. Moreover, a closer inspection of the types of businesses in this general class show that the majority of Negro businesses are restaurants. Viewing Negro business as a whole, our survey shows that a half of such enterprises provide personal and professional services to the Negro community.

Even this cursory view of the occupational status of the Negro in Harlem, as well as the analysis of the character and extent of his business enterprises, shows that he must depend mainly upon the industries, trading establishments, and other economic institutions of the larger New York community for a living. Therefore, the policies and practices of these economic institutions of the City of New York in regard to the employment of Negroes determine, in the final analysis, the economic well-being of the Negro citizens of Harlem. We shall turn our attention to this phase of the problem.

Discrimination in Employment

We shall consider first the public utilities, which have maintained a caste system in regard to the employment of Negroes. The Fifth Avenue Coach Company is so fixed in its policy of the exclusion of Negroes from employment that it refused even to discuss the question. While the officials in the other public utilities will give a polite ear to the question, their records indicate that they have systematically excluded Negro workers or restricted them to a relatively few menial jobs. The Consolidated Gas Company has only 213 Negroes among its 10,000 employees.

Practically all of these Negro workers are employed either as hallmen or porters. Likewise, among the approximately 10,000 employees of the New York Edison Company there are even fewer Negroes employed. This company employs only 65 Negroes, all of whom are confined to such menial jobs as porters, cleaners and hallmen. The same situation was found to exist in the case of the New York Telephone Company, which employs only a small number of Negroes as laborers, and in the case of the New York Railways Company, which employs about twenty-five Negroes, most of them in menial positions, out of a total of around 1,700 employees. Among the 10,000 employees of the Interborough Rapid Transit Company we found that there were about 580 Negroes employed as messengers, porters and cleaners, while the Brooklyn-Manhattan Transportation Company has a contingent of about 200 Negroes in similar positions.

In regard to the 244 Negroes among the 2,000 employees of the Independent Subway System, we shall have more to say below. The status of the Negro in the Western Union Telegraph Company has been modified to some extent during recent years through the employment of two clerks and two operators in the Harlem office; but outside of this office the Negroes employed by this corporation occupy the same menial position as colored employees in the other public utilities.

Offer Old Excuses For Discrimination

An investigation of the reasons offered by those in charge of the public utilities for discrimination against Negro workers revealed that they are the same as the excuses which have been used for nearly a century to prevent the Negro from competing on an equal basis with the whites. First, the excuse is offered by the officials of those companies that tradition and custom have restricted the employment of Negroes in positions symbolic of their inferior status in American civilization. For example, Mr. B. H. Boggs, vice-president in charge of personnel of the New York Telephone Company, did not regard the exclusion of Negroes from all positions, except a few jobs as laborers, as discrimination, but only as a customary practice. The same example was given by an official in the New York Railways Company. A second reason put forward for the exclusion of Negroes from the higher positions was that they were less efficient than white workers in similar positions.

This was the reason offered by officials in both the Consolidated Gas Company and the New York Edison Company, which had, according to their statements, employed Negro collectors at one time in Harlem. A third reason given by officials of some companies for the failure to employ Negroes was that whites and Negroes could not work in harmony. This type of excuse is represented by the statement of an official of the New York Telephone Company, who thought that the training of colored operators would require a separate school and that friction between white and colored employees would slow up the service.

Utilities' Reasons Only Rationalization

The reasons offered by the officials of the public utilities are on the whole merely rationalizations of policies and practices which have no basis in reason or fact. Undoubtedly, tradition and custom have played a part in the almost total exclusions of the Negro from all but the most menial positions.

But in a large cosmopolitan community like New York City where all races of the globe are engaged in its competitive life, custom and tradition do not present insuperable obstacles to the employment of Negroes as they would in a small community.

Negroes, contrary to traditional and customary ideas regarding their economic status, occupy positions of authority requiring intelligence and character in federal, state and municipal agencies. What peculiar circumstances, one may ask, exist in the public utilities which make it necessary to exclude the Negro or keep him in menial jobs? Moreover, in regard to the argument that Negroes and whites cannot work together harmoniously, one need only cite the public school system where white and colored teachers work together harmoniously in various parts of the city. The argument that Negro collectors are less competent than whites is unsound because it is a type of generalization concerning the moral and intellectual character of Negroes that cannot be sustained by facts. Individual Negroes may be dishonest and incompetent but this is no reason for the exclusion of the entire race from employment.

The refusal on the part of the public utilities to employ Negroes except in a few menial occupations makes them in the eyes of the people of Harlem chiefly agencies for exploiting the Negro. The Negro has no choice but to avail himself of the services of the public utilities which autocratically deny him all opportunity to share in the employment which he helps to provide other workers.

Utilities Regarded As Exploiters

While it is neither socially nor economically sound to employ Negroes or any other racial group in proportion to their importance as consumers or in areas in which they predominate, nevertheless, it may help to emphasize the

the injustice against the Negro worker by calling attention to the fact of the extent of which the Negro figures as a consumer of the services of some of these public utilities.

Even on a conservative estimate, the 50,167 Negro families in Harlem spend annually around two million dollars with the gas and electric companies and three-fourths of a million dollars with the telephone company. Yet none of the public utilities give employment to more than a few hundred Negroes who are restricted to the lowest and least remunerative forms of employment. Increasingly the Negroes of Harlem are becoming conscious of the discrimination practiced in regard to employment on the part of the public utilities. Throughout the public hearings conducted by the commission there were protests against the policy of these corporations which were held up as the chief obstacles to the economic advancement of the Negro.

Discrimination against Negro workers on the part of the public utilities is at present beyond municipal control; for in spite of their public character, the practices of these corporations represent the acts of private individuals. But these limitations do not exist in the case of the Independent Subway System which comes definitely under the jurisdiction of the municipal government. From the beginning, the Independent Subway System attempted to restrict the Negro to employment in those positions which have been traditionally regarded as Negro jobs. From evidence given before hearings conducted by the subcommittees, it appears that it was the established practice to refuse to give Negroes application blanks for any position but that of porter. Although after the Independent Subway System was placed under the civil service, this policy was modified, Negroes are still serving chiefly as porters. The relatively few Negroes who have been employed as platform men or in the booths have been restricted to the Harlem area or other areas where Negroes predominate.

In addition to these general discriminatory practices, it was brought to the attention of the commission during the course of its hearings that Negro workers who fill the so-called "Negro job" of porter are forced to suffer unnecessary hardships both in respect to pay and the conditions under which they are compelled to work. According to the schedule of pay, porters are supposed to receive from forty to fifty cents per hour. But, as far as one was able to learn from testimony given at the hearings, no porters are paid the maximum figure.

Rate of Pay Found at Minimum

The rate of pay for this position, occupied exclusively by Negroes, is less than that paid trackmen whose work requires no additional skill and incurs no greater danger. Moreover, it was also brought out in the hearings that the porters are forced to work even during the winter months in wet clothing without a room in which they might warm themselves. In fact, no place is provided for those men to change from street to work clothes, There is no choice left them but to come to and from work in their work clothes.

When the porters have complained about the lack of adequate quarters, their protests have been ignored or dismissed as frivilous. At the same time, they have been forbidden the use of the dressing rooms which are reserved for the white conductors and motormen. The complaints of the porters against these hardships cannot be dismissed on the grounds that they are inherent in the nature of their work. The hardships which the porters are compelled to endure are tantamount to discrimination against a racial group inasmuch as these discriminations are practiced against a race that is restricted to employment on this occupational level, a level which is considered proper with its general status as a race.

Discrimination against Negro workers on the part of private enterprise is shown either in the restriction of the Negro to certain menial jobs or in his total exclusion from all types of occupations. While the Negro has accepted this discrimination outside of Harlem with resignation, he has gradually developed a determination to fight it within the area which he regards as his own community. As the economic crisis became more acute, various groups began agitation for jobs in the different enterprises that draw their support from Negroes.

The demand on the part of these various groups was not simply for the menial jobs which have been traditionally given to Negroes, but for the so-called white collar jobs and other positions where intelligence and a high degree of responsibility were required. The outburst on March 19 expressed the pent-up resentment of the Negro against exclusion from all but the most menial jobs in the establishments which he supported to a large extent.

A survey of eleven of the census tracts, to which a percentage of the population is composed of Negroes, showed that 2,173, or 45.7 per cent, of the 4,730 employees in businesses were Negroes. However, since 848, or 39 per cent of the Negro employees, were in businesses conducted by Negroes, only 1,325, or a third of the employees in the businesses conducted by whites, were Negroes. Since, as we have pointed out above, the whites conduct the most substantial and important businesses, only three out of the five of the Negro employees in the businesses of this area share the fruits of the most profitable enterprises in the area.

Employment Subterfuge Revealed

Moreover, it should be borne in mind that the vast majority of these Negro employees are employed either in menial positons or in small white grocery stores and shops which have adopted this policy in order to avoid the hostility of their Negro patrons. The larger white businesses have either ignored the agitation on the part of the Negro or have adopted subterfuges. The Kress store on 125th street, where the outburst started, adopted the subterfuge of employing Negro girls at the lunch counter, claiming that it had thereby placed Negro girls on the sales force. The Negroes in Harlem readily saw through this subterfuge, as they recognized that it was strictly in keeping with tradition for Negroes to serve food, and they have continued their agitation.

Outside of Harlem the Negro is very often excluded from the very jobs in which he has traditionally found employment. Let us take first the case of the Terminal Barber Shops, a corporation which operates barber shops in various large hotels and transportation centers in Manhattan. The man in charge of the personnel work thought that it would be most extraordinary to see a Negro in a white barber shop in any capacity and confessed that he would be embarrassed if a Negro applied for a job.

This man, evidently of foreign birth and therefore never having heard that a Southern gentleman would never permit a poor white man to shave him, gave as his opinion that white people preferred white barbers, and added that the workers would object to Negro barbers. It is needless to comment on such rationalizations which are used to exclude the Negro from employment. The exclusion of Negro waiters, cooks and other classes of employees from the hotels would probably be supported by similar types of reasoning. Our survey of 393 hotels of all types in the Borough of Manhattan, showed that 238, or 60 per cent, had no Negro employees. Thus the Negro workers, for no other reason than because of the arbitrary practice or prejudice of hotel managers, is denied employment in a field in which he once found a steady source of income.

Employment in City's Large Stores

On the whole, the stores and other types of business enterprises outside of Harlem may be divided into two classes in regard to their policy in regard to the employment of Negroes: those that employ Negroes in menial positions and those that employ no Negroes at all. For example, a representative of the first class in Macy's, which has employed Negroes for many years, with Negroes serving as elevator starters, escalator attendants, and in the cafeteria and tea rooms. On the other hand, there is Gimbel's, which excludes Negroes from any type of employment.

Most of the Negroes employed downtown occupy jobs as elevator operators, porters and to a less extent as messengers. While some of the business establishments excluding Negroes from employment in their downtown establishments seemingly attempt to compensate for their discrimination by employing them in Harlem, the insurance companies, with thousands of policy holders in Harlem, are adamant in their policy of refusing to employ Negro agents even in Harlem. First among such companies is the Metropolitan Life Insurance Company, with over a among the Negroes in Harlem.

This company attempts to excuse its policy on the ground that white agents produce better results. But the experience of Negro companies, which depend solely upon Negro agents, refutes this charge. The same is true of the Workingman's Co-operative Association of the United Insurance League of New York, of whose 13,020 policy holders (as of December 31, 1934) about 95 per cent are Negroes, 5,000 being in Harlem. The secretary-treasurer of the company gave as his excuse for not employing Negro agents that, since the average Negro family consulted the insurance agent on matters other than insurance, they preferred white agents. The president of the Golden Eagle Life and Accident Association, with headquarters in Brooklyn, offered a similar excuse for not employing Negro agents. Between 8 and 9 per cent of the policy holders in this company are Negroes and about half of them live in Harlem.

No study of discrimination against Negroes in employment could be complete without a consideration of the discriminatory practices of the labor unions. In spite of the repeated resolutions by the American Federation of Labor at its annual meetings to the effect that it discountenanced racial discrimination, it's pious pronouncements have had little effect upon the practices of its constituent national and international unions.

Although only a few of those national and international unions which limit the employment of Harlem Negroes have constitutional or ritual provisions excluding Negro workers, the actual practices of these unions are as effective as constitutional restrictions. For example, an apprenticeship requirement for admission to a union may very effectively exclude Negro members. Take for example the International Brotherhood of Electrical Workers, Local Union No. 3, with a membership of 6,000, none of whom are Negroes. Although this union has no provisions concerning Negro membership, the seven years' apprenticeship requirement excludes Negroes as members as effectively as the constitutional provision in the charter of the Commercial Telegraphers' Union, which states that only white persons may become members. Sometimes the union excuse the absence of Negro members on the grounds that no Negroes were in the particular trade or occupation which they represent.

Negroes Not Wanted in Many Unions

For example, the Railway Express Employees, Local 608, of the International Brotherhood of Teamsters and Chauffeurs, does not have a single Negro among its 2,000 members for the reason, they claim, that the Railway Express Agency does not employ Negroes as chauffeurs, helpers or stablemen. The same reason was offered by the president of the New York Newspaper Printing Pressmen and Assistants' Union of North America, for the fact that not one of the union's 3,000 members was a Negro.

As a matter of fact, some of the unions attempt to limit their membership, especially during periods of unemployment, and this applies to the white worker as well as the Negro. The International Alliance of Bill Pasters and Billers of America, Local No. 2, with a membership of 300, accomplishes this through the high initiation fee. Since this fee is $500 one can readily understand why no Negro is a member slthough it was stated that they would accept a Negro if he applied for membership.

Bartender's Union Local No. 3, with 1,100 members, according to the secretary, had never thought of organizing Negro bartenders, since they are so few, into a separate local. So far as taking them into Local No. 3 he did not know whether the men would like it and such a step would call "for a lot of other considerations." It is quite unnecessary to catalogue the various reasons off red to explain why Negroes are not members of the various unions. The available figures on the membership of Negroes in the various locals in New York City are probably the best indication of the policies of the different unions.

In the various locals representing the building trades, there are less than 1,000 Negroes in a membership close to 40,000. In the clothing and textile industries about 6,704 Negroes are to be found among a membership of over 150,000 in the various unions. Almost all of these Negro union members are in the International Ladies' Garment Workers' Union. Negro members are excluded entirely from the clerical unions. With the exception of the Association of Workers in the Public Relief Agencies, the Postal Workers' locals, and Sanitary Chauffeurs, Negroes are practically excluded from the unions representing public service. We find practically the same situation in regard to the field of amusements and the professions if we exclude the American Federation of Musicians, Local 802, which has over 86 per cent of the Negro union members in this general field.

Union Policy Against Negroes

The general policy of many of these unions was probably unconsciously expressed by the representative of one when he said that, since there had been no strikes, his union had not thought of organizing Negro workers. This statement taken together with that above of the secretary of the bartenders' union sums up the situation which we see illustrated in the case of the Motion Picture Operators' Union, Local 306. When the Negro motion picture operators organized and applied to this local for membership, they were offered a limited membership, that is, they were to pay the regular dues and be subject to the same rules as other members of the union but they had no vote and were not to attend the meetings.

The Negro operators naturally refused. When they were later admitted to full membership, the membership proved simply a means of controlling the Negro worker. He was assigned only to work in the theatres in the Negro section of Harlem. When work became slack during the present depression, other forms of discrimination were practiced. The white members of the union are given a chance to earn a regular week's pay at least twice a month at a salary around $51 per week, while the colored operators are given only one week's work at a theatre in Harlem and are paid the $18 weekly unemployment benefit out of union funds for the remainder of the time.

This extraordinary record of discrimination against the Harlem Negro in the matter of employment accounts to a large extent for the continuous impoverishment of the more than 200,000 citizens of this area of New York City. It represents a denial of the fundamental rights of a people to a livelihood. The amount of charity, good will, social privileges, or political freedom can compensate for the enforced idleness and poverty of the citizens of this (sic) community. The low economic status of the Negro in Harlem is basic to every other problem in the community.

It is idle to reflect upon the large numbers of Negroes unemployed or their poor housing conditions, or their petty thefts, while the right to work at lawful occupations is denied them. The social costs of such a policy may not be apparent but, nevertheless, they are a constant drain on the economic resources of the larger community. Moreover, in times of stress when relief fails to compensate for systematic exclusion from legitimate work, we have such recurrences as the outbreak of March 19.

CHAPTER IV

The Relief Situation

In the foregoing chapter we have seen how racial discrimination against the Negro on the part of the public utilities, private enterprises, and the labor unions has narrowed the field of his employment and denied him the chance for economic security that other groups enjoy. This has naturally produced a state of perpetual unemployment and dependence upon welfare agencies. Although it is impossible to obtain a precise measure of the extent of dependency during normal times, statistics from the Charity Organization Society throw some light on the situation.

For example, during the fiscal year 1927-1928, this organization had 592 Negro families under care and rendered incidental services to many more. These 592 Negro families comprised 24.7 per cent of all "under care" families in the area north of 98th street and on the west side down to 46th street. The proportion of Negro families "under care," was, from 1924 and onward, between 20 and 25 per cent; but began to mount as the economic crisis approached. Since the fiscal year, 1930, the proportion of Negro families "under care" has remained between 40 and 45 per cent of the total.

It is even more difficult to get reliable figures on the extent of unemployment among Negroes during normal times. According to the federal census on unemployment in 1930, before the full effects of the present economic crisis made themselves felt, there were in the Borough of Manhattan alone 8,102 Negroe males and 4,006 Negro females able to work and seeking employment who were out of jobs, not including nearly a thousand men and women who had been laid off without pay.

Difficult to Get Adequate Figures

Since the census, which undoubtedly gave an inadequate picture of unemployment, was made, the depression has become more acute. This is reflected in the number of applicants, nearly all of whom are Negroes, who have sought employment at the Harlem office of the State Employment Service. During the year 1926 there were 5,609 applicants; this number increasing to 28,279 during the year 1930. Although the number declined to 17,434 in 1934, there is no reason to believe that this decrease has been due to a comparable increase in the number of Negroes employed. We can get a more accurate picture of the present situation from the figures on the number of Negro families on relief in the Harlem area alone. During the first week of September in 1933, there were 24,293 Negro families, exclusive of unattached men and women, on the relief rolls. On the basis of the 1934 census of the Housing Authority, these 24,293 families constituted 43.2 per cent of the Negro families in the Harlem area.

Even before the present Home Relief Bureau was set up, the Negroes of Harlem made complaints against the manner in which the relief situation was handled. These complaints were due in part to the attempt to shunt all needy in Harlem. But, more specifically, the Negroes of Harlem objected to the red tape and subterfuges which stood in the way of their getting assistance.

Then, too, there were protests against placing a white woman in charge on the assumption, hinted if not openly avowed, that no Negro was capable of assuming such a responsibility. The setting up of the Home Relief Bureau did not bring an end to these complaints. In fact, as the economic crisis became acute, complaints against the Home Relief Bureau and the Works Division increased in volume and hostility of the community towards these agencies became more open.

1. The Question of Negro Personnel

In spite of numerous denials, the Home Relief Bureau, at least in the beginning of its work, followed the pattern set by the community at large in the appointment of Negro personnel. No amount of sophistry about administrative technicalities can convince a sane person that the Home Relief Bureau has considered Negroes only on the basis of their individual merits while other institutions, as we have shown in the preceding chapters, have nearly always taken into consideration the race of the Negro in giving him employment. The white people in the Home Relief Bureau reflect more or less all the current prejudices concerning the Negro's place in society and it is therefore idle for them to represent either themselves or their actions as being entirely uninfluenced by these prejudices. Moreover, there are many southern white people in the Home Relief Bureau who are just as determined to "keep the Negro in his place" in New York City as they were in the southern communities from which they come. Then, too, when it has come to a question of either offending these southerners or insulting and keeping Negroes from the higher positions, very often the prejudices of these southerners have carried more weight than the merits of Negroes. Naturally, it is difficult to prove discrimination against the Negro when there are so many technical devices at the disposal of those in charge to make their actions appear just and impartial. Nevertheless, we have not been compelled to rely upon deductions from what is known concerning the general attitudes of whites in the Home Relief Bureau for our conclusions. Enough reliable evidence is available to substantiate the charge that discrimination was shown in the placement of Negro personnel in the Home Relief Bureau since its inception. The following table gives the changes which have taken place in respect to the Negro personnel between January 5, 1935, and July 1, 1935, for the T.E.R.A. From this table it appears that the number of Negroes increased significantly in the investigator and service groups between January 5 and July 1 of 1935. We do not

TABLE II

NUMBER OF NEGROES ON THE STAFF OF THE HOME RELIEF BUREAU
CLASSIFIED ACCORDING TO PAYROLL GROUP

WORK DIVISION STAFF

Payroll Group	January 5, 1935	July 1, 1935
Investigator Group	362	495
Clerical Group	382	361
Service Group	4	105
Others	3	22
Total	701	973
Percentage of Entire Work Division Payroll	7.3	8.6

T. E. R. A. STAFF

Payroll Group	April 1, 1935	Payroll Group	July 1, 1935
Administrative Staff	3	Supervisors in D.C.	13
Office Staff	0	Medical Social Workers	
Case Work Staff	63	Nutritionists in D.C.	6
		Aides, etc., in D.C.	72
		Others	2
Total	70	Total	93
Percentage of entire T.E.R.A. payroll	6.9	Percentage of entire T.E.R.A. payroll	8.4

have any other evidence on the increase in the Negro personnel in the Home Relief Bureau than that which is given in the following table. Although the

TABLE III

NUMBER OF NEGRO MEMBERS OF THE HOME RELIEF BUREAU STAFF, AS OF JULY 1, 1935, WHO WERE ON STAFF IN 1934, 1333, 1932 and 1931

WORK DIVISION STAFF

Payroll Group	July 1, 1935	1934	1933	1932	1931
Service Group.............	105	49	17	3	0
Clerical Group............	361	256	86	31	10
Investigator Group........	495	338	107	27	9
Others....................	22	19	6	2	1
Total..................	973	662	216	63	20

T. E. R. A. STAFF

Payroll Group	July 1, 1935	1934	1933	1932	1931
Supervisors in D.C.	13	13	10	7	5
Medical Social Workers and Nutritionists in D.C.	6	4	0	0	0
Aides, etc., in D.C.	72	67	40	16	6
Others....................	2	2	1	0	0
Total..................	93	86	51	23	11

figures given in Table III actually give only the length of service of present Negro members of the Home Relief Bureau, it serves as a fairly good index to the history of the Negro in the Bureau. In view of the limited employment opportunities for Negroes, especially educated Negroes, it is unlikely that many of them have voluntarily left the Home Relief Bureau. Nor, is there any reason to believe that many of them have been dropped by the Bureau or that there was a greater proportion of Negroes in the higher positions in the past than at present. Therefore, it seems reasonable to conclude from this table that only a negligible number of Negroes were employed by the Bureau when it began its work. Moreover, this conclusion is in accord with the complaints that were made against the Bureau.

Employ More Negroes On Home Relief Staff

Further inspection of this table reveals that the number of Negroes in the Bureau in 1934 showed an increase of 200 per cent over the number in mounting (sic). Although in 1934 the number of Negroes in the Bureau had become fairly large, the number rose very sharply--nearly 50 per cent--in the first six months of 1935. While these figures do not indicate the number of Negroes employed in the Home Relief Bureau for each of the years, they confirm what has been generally charged against the Bureau; namely, that at the outset it adopted on the whole the same policy as the public utilities and private enterprises in excluding all but a relatively few Negroes from employment. This was admitted by Mr. Corsi in his testimony before the commission on April 27, 1935, when he stated that when he took office he did not think Negroes were fairly represented on the staff.

According to the statement of July 1, 1933, the 1,066 Negro employees in the Bureau constituted about 8.6 per cent of the entire staff. Representatives of the Home Relief Bureau have emphasized the fact that the percentage of Negroes on the staff exceeded the percentage of Negroes in the general population. But, in determining whether Negroes were discriminated against in the appointments to the personnel of the Bureau, other factors are of greater consequence. The important question at issue is whether Negroes were given positions and were promoted on the same basis as other persons. An analysis of the figures furnished by the Bureau show that Negroes were not given supervisory positions nor positions which might designate as strategic. First, we observe in Table IV, that Negroes figure most prominently in the service group, comprising porters, watchmen, matrons, guards and messengers.

TABLE IV

MEMBERS OF THE HOME RELIEF BUREAU AND T. E. R. A. STAFF AS OF JULY 1, 1935, CLASSIFIED ACCORDING TO COLOR AND PAYROLL GROUPS

WORK DIVISION STAFF

Payroll Group	White	Colored	Other	Total
Investigator Group	4,106	493	1	4,602
Clerical Group	4,978	151	2	5,331
Service Group	740	105	0	845
Others	475	22	0	497
Total	10,299	975	3	11,275
Percentage Distribution	91.4	8.6	0.0	100.0

T. E. R. A. STAFF

	White	Colored	Other	Total
Supervisors in D.C.	231	13	0	244
Medical Social Workers and Nutritionists in D.C.	71	6	0	77
Aides, Intake and Receptionists in D.C.	376	72	2	648
Others	128	2	0	140
Total	1,014	93	2	1,100

They constitute 14.2 per cent of this entire type of service in the Home Relief Bureau. On the other hand, if we consider the supervisors' group, we find that only 5.6 per cent of this group is composed of Negroes. The supervisory group includes nine assistant supervisors, one case supervisor, one office manager, and the two administrators who were appointed recently in two of the Harlem precincts. The absence of Negroes in supervisory positions can be explained neither as a chance phenomenon nor as a result of their lack of training. For example, in one case at least a young colored woman with professional social work training and experience who was found qualified for a supervisory position was told that she had better accept an inferior position because she could not be appointed to a supervisory position.

When she was first interviewed for the position and found to possess superior training, the official in charge was seemingly ignorant of the policy in regard to Negroes; for it was only after a whispered consultation with her colleagues that she gave the Negro woman the "friendly" advice about accepting an inferior position. This same colored woman afterwards trained inexperienced white women with a meager education for positions equal to her own and qualified them for promotion. At the hearings conducted by the commission the officials in the Home Relief Bureau attempted to explain the few Negroes in supervisory positions by claiming to be training Negroes for the occupancy of such positions in the future.

The classification, "other" in Table IV needs special attention. Under this apparently innocuous division are concealed two very important occupations. It will be observed that 22 or only 4.8 of the 476 occupations classified under "others" are filled by Negroes. Glancing back at Table II we find that on Jan. 1, 1935, only five Negroes were in such occupations.

Negroes Not in Strategic Posts

In this division classified as "others" we find, in addition to nurses and receptionists, two of the most important occupations in the Home Relief Bureau: that of insurance advisor and that of occupational clerk. When the statement of July 1, 1935, is analysed, it is found that there were only four Negro insurance advisors and five Negro occupational clerks in the entire

Home Relief set-up. Thus from both of these strategic positions in the Home Relief Bureau, Negroes were practically excluded. The position of insurance advisor, in spite of the formal rules laid down concerning the adjustment of insurance for clients, was one in which one could exercise considerable discretion. Whereas competent Negroes could have carried out the aim of this office with sympathy and understanding, often white insurance advisors with no sympathy or understanding of the Negro's plight in regard to his small insurance handled these clients ruthlessly. The position of occupational clerk was even more important so far as the Negro was concerned for it was through this office that systematic discrimination in work relief was carried on.

Discrimination in the appointment of Negro personnel to the Home Relief Bureau reflected the policy of the New York community. Superior Negro men and women with business and professional experience were placed under white officials who were obviously inferior to them. In one case a white official of Southern birth boasted that he knew how to handle "niggers." In fact, some of the officials were more concerned in preserving what they thought proper race relations than in seeing that their clients were properly looked after.

This was due to the fact that a large percentage of the workers in the Bureau paid little attention to traditional ideas concerning the Negro and thus incurred the displeasure of those officials who were anxious to keep the Negro in his place. In view of the conditions under which the Negro personnel worked they displayed remarkable restraint and emotional balance.

2. The Administration of Home Relief

Numerous charges have been made by both white and colored people in Harlem that discrimination has been shown towards Negroes in the administration of Home Relief. It is obvious that it would be an almost impossible task to follow up and verify the numerous charges that have been made in this regard. Where there has been so much distrust concerning the impartial functioning of an institution, there are likely to be many baseless rumors concerning discrimination.

Moreover, it is quite possible that delays due to routine investigations and the refusal of aid to applicants ineligible for relief should have become the basis for charges of racial discrimination. On the other hand, since the procedure in administering home relief was standardized to a large extent and since many of the investigators of Negro families were themselves Negroes, it is difficult to see how racial discrimination could have figured greatly in home relief. Therefore, it is quite possible that many of the charges of racial discrimination were due to the same causes responsible for complaints made by other races (?).

In our investigation of the charges of racial discrimination we have examined the confidential weekly statistical reports of the Home Relief Bureau over a period of six months relative to expenditures, the allowance for special diets, and the number of cases closed. In regard to expenditures, it was found that the home relief precincts in the Negro section of Manhattan overspent their budget allowances as frequently and to the same extent as other precincts in Manhattan and in other sections of New York City. Moreover, as far as one was able to determine from the figures, neither the average amount of relief per case nor the average expenditure according to the number of persons per case shows any discrimination against the distinctively Negro precincts.

Discrimination Not Always Shown

The same was true from an inspection of the proportion of the budget spent by the various precincts for such individual items as food, shelter, fuel, light and clothing, as compared with the proportion of cases and persons receiving relief in these precincts. In respect to cases receiving special diet allowances, there was no indication of discrimination against Negro precincts either as to the proportion of cases or the excess cost per person. When an examination was made of the statistics on the number and percentage of cases closed in the various precincts, it did not appear that there was any reason for assuming that cases in precincts predominantly Negro have been closed to a greater extent than in other precincts. Therefore, so far as those statistics for the period from May to October, 1935, are an index to whether an impartial attitude was maintained in the distribution of relief, there is no indication of discrimination against the Negro precincts.

However, when one examines the statistics on complaints received by the adjustment service from the various precincts, one finds that for the period, October 9, 1935, to October 31, 1935, a significantly higher percentage of complaints, based upon the size of the various case loads, came from the Harlem regional division than from any other division. During this period 579 complaints or 26 per 1,000 cases came from Harlem, as compared with 12.6 to 14.1 for the Brooklyn divisions and 14.1 for the Bronx. The only division that approached the Harlem division was the East Manhattan and Richmond division with 23.3 complaints per 1,000 cases. While the Harlem division showed a higher complaint rate than any other division, the classification of the complaints in this division showed practically the same distribution as in the other divisions. In the Harlem division 46.4 per cent of the complaints charged an inadequate relief budget; 22.8 per cent that relief checks and vouchers had been delayed; 20.5 per cent that relief had been denied; 4.7 per cent that investigation had been delayed; 2.8 per cent that investigator was unsatisfactory; 2.1 per cent that treatment in the district office was unsatisfactory; and 0.7 per cent charging discrimination.

Although we are not in a position to say to what extent there was justification for a comparatively larger number of complaints from the Harlem division than any other division, from an examination of the complaints and the action taken in two of the precincts in the Harlem division, it appears that these complaints were often justified.

Most Requests Got Attention

For example, in Precinct 32, for the month of October, 1935, 70 of the 80 WPA clients, who requested food, were granted their requests; and in 73 cases of 80 WPA clients requesting clothing and shoes, the requests were granted or orders were placed for clothing and shoes. In this same precinct for the same period, 102 home relief clients complained that their tickets were late. According to the analysis of this precinct, in 32 of these cases it was the fault of the Home Relief Bureau. In Precinct 26, during the period from October 6, 1935, to November 5, 1935, in response to 41 complaints concerning delay in receiving food, one request was granted, in one case, the investigator was in the field with relief, one transfer had been delayed, and one replacement was issued.

These two precincts have been chosen simply because they were supplied by the Home Relief Bureau and therefore give some insight into the nature of the complaints and the action taken on them. It should be borne in mind with reference to both the analysis of the statistics on the complaints for the various divisions and the situation in these two precincts that our information on the Harlem situation deals with a period subsequent to the outbreak of March 19 and the hearings which the commission held on the relief situation. We are not in a position to say whether or not the relief situation in Harlem has improved during the past year as the status of Negro personnel has done during this period. However, it is proper that certain observations should be made even on the basis of this limited data. It is undoubtedly true that there have been many hardships endured by the citizens of Harlem on relief. In some cases the more thorough and sympathetic investigations of private agencies have shown Negro clients to be eligible for relief when they have been refused by the Home Relief Bureau because of such technicalities as the establishment of legal residence.

Some Failed to Get Benefit of Doubt

In some cases it appeared that a Negro was simply not given benefit of the doubt, an act on the part of the Home Relief Bureau that only increased the widespread human misery in this area. Then, too, too little sympathetic understanding has been shown towards the difficulties which these people, only slightly acquainted with the complexities of urban existence, have had to encounter. It is not only inexcusable but cruel to force a widow and her three children to subsist for months on a fortnightly allowance of two small cans of milk and two cans of beef, because it is suspected that she has a balance from her husband's meager death benefit, which has almost entirely been confiscated by the undertaker. Yet it is true that such things have happened to relief clients in Harlem.

Discrimination in Work Relief

While there may be some question about discrimination against Negroes in home relief, it is an incontrovertible fact that systematic discrimination has been carried on against the Negro in work relief. As a matter of fact, most of the complaints brought against the administration of relief in Harlem has been in regard to work relief. The same type of discrimination which was protested in the assignment of Negroes by the New York branch of the N.A.A.C.P. of twelve building projects under the PWA, there were only 41 Negro bricklayers and carpenters employed on those projects, which included the Harlem Hospital with 14, the Parcel Post Building with 3, the school buildings with a total of 10, Radio City with 10, the Bronx County Court House and the Manhattan Armory with 2 each. Testimony given before the commission on April 20, 1935, showed that about a week prior to that date a gang of Negro riveters were sent from the Harlem office of the State Employment Service to a project of the American Bridge Construction Company. The foreman told the Negro workers that they were not wanted and that Negro workers were never employed. Such instances of discrimination, which have been numerous, have been referred to the administrative heads of the State Employment Service without any results.

To see that there has been no change in this policy of discrimination, one needs only to read the daily records of unused labor calls for clearance of the New York State Employment Service, which is affiliated with the United States Employment Service. An analysis of those reports for the last three weeks of October, 1935, showed the following: Of 295 calls for men, the reports specified that 271 whites, 11 Jews, 7 white or colored men, 5 colored men and 1 Indian or Filipino were wanted. Of 201 calls for women, the reports specified that 163 whites, 7 Jews, 17 white or colored women, and 14 colored women were wanted. The majority of the calls requesting either white or colored men and women or just colored men and women were for jobs in domestic service. Only 8 of the total of 41 such calls were for what would be classified as skilled occupations.

For a well-balanced and impartial statement concerning discrimination against Negroes in Work Relief we may quote from the conclusions of a report presented December 5, 1935, by the division of information and review of the TERA concerning discrimination against Negroes on Work Relief Project 33 in New York City:

> "The evidence gathered by this inquiry substantiated four of the five specific complaints on the part of the Negroes regarding discrimination in lay-offs. The charge that Negroes with dependents were dismissed while white workers with no dependents were restrained (sic), was disproved by the inquiry."

Find Discrimination in Lay-Offs

> "The injustices in lay-offs which occurred, namely, a disproportionate number of Negroes laid off, the dismissal of qualified and efficient workers and of those with a large number of dependents, the ignoring of seniority of service and the possibilities of misclassification were traceable almost solely to the haphazard and unscientific policy of dismissals which entrusted the decision to the supervisors and squad leaders.
>
> The lack of efficiency ratings and records and proper review by superior officials of the Works Division enabled various squad leaders, prejudiced against the Negro race as a whole, or against Negro subordinates who had expressed resentment against previous discriminatory tactics by their supervisors, to discharge highly trained Negro workers possessing superior technical knowledge.
>
> Five of the seven specific charges of racial discrimination during work on Project 33 were found to be valid by the inquiry. Such discriminatory tactics as segregation of work locations in Negro districts, retention of superior workers in subordinate positions, assignment of less desirable work, intimidation and spying upon a Negro informant, and a hypocritical and domineering attitude on the part of certain supervisors, proved to be the major occasions of the friction which developed in a number of squads on Project 33.

In several instances this friction was traceable to a sense of inferiority which white squad leaders experience in the presence of higher qualified colored workers under them. This feeling of inadequacy manifested itself in domineering attitudes, brusqueness, personal abuse against colored workers, blanket condemnation of the work habits of the whole Negro race, overloading of tasks, and finally, where no scientific race doomed 'congenitally inferior.'"

Voice Indifference to Complaints

"Moreover, lack of impartiality in the evidence at hearings before the chief supervisors and Works Division officials to consider charges of Negro discrimination, and the inexcusable delay in reinstating Mr. Prout, admittedly discharged through an error of the Home Relief office, indifference to complaints voiced by Negroes against certain officials of the Works Division and Home Relief Administration, raises grave suspicion of discrimination."

The same type of racial discrimination was continued under the Works Progress Administration. In the first place, a disproportionately large number of Negroes were given a wrong classification, generally that of laborer. As a matter of fact, the occupational clerk in one precinct refused to refer Negroes on any jobs. The second type of discrimination is due to the refusal on the part of those in charge of projects to accept qualified Negroes who are sent to them.

Strange as it may seem, the American Museum of Natural History has been conspicuous for its refusal to accept qualified Negroes on its projects. This scientific organization has resorted to such obvious subterfuges as pretending that space was lacking or that the qualifying official was out of town. Let us take the example of a young Negro woman, qualified as a bacteriologist, who was sent to the American Museum of Natural History:

"Miss L. was sent to the Intake Bureau at 245 East Twenty-fifth street, where she received a slip to go to Mr. X at the American Museum of Natural History. She filled out the application blank and stood in line with other persons, all of whom were white. Mr. X, on his way out to lunch, seeing her, picked her out of the line and questioned her concerning her education and experience. He told her that she had just the qualification which he wanted and that she should come back the next day. On the next day she was sent to the Botanical Gardens to work on fungi and molds. The man in charge there had no opening for her but wanted Dr. I. to take a man from his staff in order that an opening might be made, and gave her a note to that effect. In the meantime, Dr. I., who had changed his attitude, refused to make the transfer and gave Miss L. a slip stating that the qualifying official was out of town and would not return until two months later."

Letters Reveal Discrimination

As evidence of the type of discrimination that is practiced by the officials in charge of the Works Progress Administration we present the following memoranda from a precinct in Harlem concerning Negro workers who were refused assignment on projects:

Case No. 23375.

On 2/23/35 Mr. E. was referred as an electrician's helper. On 9/25/35 he was offered a job by the WPA as a laborer at Bear Mt., which he refused, because he witnessed a number of others being placed as electrician's helpers at the same time that he was rejected on the basis of "over quota."

Case No. 18337.

On 2/12/35 Mr. C. was referred as cement mason, at which time he was rejected because of "over-quota." At this time Mr. C. claims he witnessed others being assigned as masons, plasterers, etc. Mr. C. was offered work as a laborer, which he refused. He insisted upon being assigned as a mason, as stated on his referral slip. He finally (9/18/35) received his correct assignment, after refusing to accept work other than listed on the referral.

Case No. 707715.

On 10/2/35 Mr. G. was referred as a "painter." Ten years' experience. 10/3/35 disqualified as painter; placed as laborer.

Case No. 777443.

On 10/7/35 Mr. C. was referred as "auto mechanic." Ten years' experience. Disqualified as such. Referred as laborer. Mr. C. refused laborer's job.

Case No. 707439.

On 10/10/35 Mr. S. was referred as "newspaper man." Had two years' experience as reporter, Springfield, Mass., Daily News. Disqualified. Advised five years' experience necessary.

We are aware that in the above five cases which we have presented it may be claimed that racial discrimination did not influence the behavior of those who refused Negro workers places on projects. Therefore, in order that there will be no doubt concerning the policy of the Works Progress Administration in the assignment of Negroes on projects, we submit the following two memoranda, which show definitely that Negro workers are treated as a separate racial group:

Ming, Eunice, 114 W. 120th St., Luncheon Manager, August 22, 1935. Project Number 189, old 1058. Requisition Number 244.
Quota for colored work filled. (Report of qualifying officer, Board of Education). (Signed) A. BROWN.

Glans, New Zealand. Senior Investigator. August 21, 1935. Project Number 119 (1597X). Requisition Number 528.
Rejected. Quota filled (on colored investigators). (Signed) A. BROWN.
Project: Educational Status of Young People. Foreman: Edna B. Stair. 924 Broadway, 3d floor.

The above cases of racial discrimination are not isolated instances, but are typical of the practices against which Negroes have complained.

Work Relief in General

Some attempts have been made to disprove the existence of racial discrimination in work relief by citing the fact that a larger proportion of Negroes are on work relief than their relative numbers in the city's population would warrant. In regard to this contention, we wish to state, first, that racial discrimination is shown by the fact that Negroes are assigned chiefly to menial jobs and are given an inferior status when, by training and experience, they merit different types of appointments. Moreover, it should also be emphasized that the disproportionate number of Negroes on work relief is due in large measure to the very type of racial discrimination which the Works Progress Administration has adopted. Thus, the Negro worker finds himself in a vicious circle. Discrimination on the part of private and public enterprises causes large numbers of Negroes to become dependent upon relief; but when the relief administration sets up work projects, they are denied the work for which their training and experience fit them. It appears, as we have shown above, that justice has only been done the Negro when he has been a recipient of direct relief; since both as a member of the staff of the Home Relief Bureau and as a relief client seeking work, he has been systematically discriminated against.

CHAPTER V

The Housing Problem

Next to the problem of securing a livelihood, finding a suitable place to live constitutes the most serious problem of the Harlem Negro. The houses in the section of Harlem inhabited by the Negro were built not only for another race, but what is more important, for a group on a different economic level, and consisting of families and households of an entirely different composition from those which now occupy these dwellings. But the Negro had to take what he found and spread out as far as he was permitted.

When we consider the fact that within the past twenty-five years the Negro population in Harlem has increased over 600 per cent, it is not surprising that Harlem is one of the most densely populated sections of New York City. In the Harlem area the density of the population varies considerably from one census tract to another. In the majority of the tracts occupied by Negroes, the density ranges from 150 to 450 persons per acre. On the whole, this is similar to the variation found on the lower East Side. However, one block in Harlem, between 138th and 139th streets and Seventh and Lenox avenues, has a density of 620 persons per acre, the highest in the entire city. Economic and racial barriers have held the Negro population within certain limits, thereby making the Negro at the same time the victim of overcrowding and high rentals.

1. Physical Aspects of Housing in Harlem

The dwellings in Harlem, like the majority of the dwellings in Manhattan, are exceedingly old. In the eleven census tracts, in the heart of Harlem, in which Negro families constitute from 90 to practically 100 per cent of the families, we find that 84.2 per cent of the residential structures were built thirty-five or more years ago and 11.6 per cent have been standing from twenty to thirty-four years. There are in this area over 25,000 Negro families or about 45 per cent of all the Negro families in the entire Harlem community.

In Table V below the residential structures in this area, Area I, may be compared in respect in age with similar structures in Areas II and III into which the Negro population has spread east of Amsterdam avenue. Area IV in which Negro families constitute less than 5 per cent of the total, comprises the section of Harlem north of 98th street and, with the exception of one census tract, east of Park Avenue. Because of its general economic and social character this almost entirely white area furnishes a better area for comparison with the other three areas containing the bulk of the Negro population than the almost entirely white area to the west of the Negro community.

TABLE V

PERCENTAGE DISTRIBUTION OF STRUCTURES ACCORDING TO AGE IN AREAS COMPRISING CENSUS TRACTS GROUPED ACCORDING TO PERCENTAGE OF NEGRO FAMILIES IN TRACTS.

	Census Tracts in Which of Total Families Negro Families Constitute			
Age of Structures	90 Per Cent and Over Area I	76 to 89 Per Cent Area II	40 to 75 Per Cent Area III	Under 5 Per Cent Area IV
Less than 10 years	2.7	0.7	0.9	0.7
10 - 19 years	1.4	2.7	1.8	1.0
20 - 34 years	11.6	14.4	16.2	8.5
35 years and over	84.2	82.1	80.9	89.7
Total	99.9	99.9	99.8	99.9

From the above table, it is seen that in Areas II and III with smaller proportions of Negro families than Area I the structures are not as old as those in Area I. On the other hand, Area IV has 5.5 per cent more residential structures thirty-five years of age and over than the distinctly Negro area, Area I. We can obtain further information on the condition of the residential structures in Harlem by inspection of Table VI, in which the dwellings are compared in the four areas relative to their condition in Area I. On the

TABLE VI

PERCENTAGE DISTRIBUTION OF RESIDENTIAL STRUCTURES ACCORDING TO CONDITIONS IN AREAS COMPRISING CENSUS TRACTS GROUPED ACCORDING TO PERCENTAGE OF NEGRO FAMILIES IN TRACTS.

Condition of Structures	Census Tracts in Which of Total Families Negro Families Constitute			
	90 Per Cent Area I	76 to 89 Per Cent Area II	40 to 75 Per Cent Area III	Under 5 Per Cent Area IV
First Class	16.0	16.0	17.3	12.0
Second Class	62.8	68.5	64.1	59.3
Third Class	19.1	14.5	13.7	28.0
Fourth Class	2.0	1.0	4.7	2.6
Total	99.9	100.0	99.8	99.9

contrary, in the first three areas, I, II and III, where the bulk of the Negro population is located, about the same percentage of the structures are in good or those needing minor repairs comprise a larger percentage of the structures than dwellings in a smaller condition in Area I. (sic) On the contrary, we find a smaller percentage of third class residential structures, or those needing major repairs, in the Areas II and III. Area IV has a smaller proportion of first class dwellings than other areas, the difference being compensated for by those in third class condition. From the table it does not appear that the preponderance of fourth class dwellings, or those structurally defective, are closely associated with the concentration of Negroes, although local surveys indicate that Negroes occupy the worst houses in Areas II and III.

The figures give only in abstract outlines a general picture of the physical aspects of housing in Harlem. In order for one to get an understanding of the significance of these figures, one must see the concrete reality which is presented to the eye. Let us turn to a verbal description of one of the census tracts in Area I.

"About 87 per cent of the families in this tract are Negro. The dwellings in the tract were built during the turn of the century. About 12 per cent of them are vacant. The occupied apartments in the dwellings have a median of $58.54. The majority of the dwellings on the four streets running east and west between Eighth and St. Nicholas Avenues and Lenox Avenue are brown stone private dwellings. Most of these dwellings, showing the effects of age, are rented with kitchen facilities to roomers. Several of these dwellings have signs 'for white only' though the number of whites in the area is fast dwindling. In a few of these old private dwellings one finds quiet marooned white families that have stubbornly remained in order to avoid financial losses. In spite of the sign 'respectable people only,' on some of these dwellings, many of the private dwellings in this area are used for prostitution. When a police radio car stopped in one of these streets, considerable uneasiness on the part of the residents became apparent.

"In several of the blocks there are old law tenements, some with furnished apartments. Most of the streets are dirty and congested with children and loiterers. In the afternoons garbage cans, with their contents still uncollected, may be seen in front of the houses. In the midst of this general decay and depravity there stands a school with behavior problems reflecting the character of the community. The three avenues are of the same character as the cross streets. The private houses on Lenox Avenue are used for churches, restaurants, funeral parlors and other businesses. On Seventh and Eighth Avenues, most of the houses are old law tenements. Some of these old law tenements are fast becoming dilapidated. In one of these dilapidated tenements, still inhabited though condemned, 60 per cent of the people are on relief. The tenants in this building had become so depraved through the use of alcohol and narcotics that relief workers, after being menaced on several occasions, were afraid to enter the house. Most of the old tenements on Eighth Avenue are occupied by whites of Irish decent."

Resorting once more to the statistical picture of Area I, we find that in this area over 1,200 or about 6 per cent of the occupied family quarters are without central heating; over 2,300 or about 12 per cent are without hot water; and 722 or nearly 4 per cent are without indoor toilets.

If fromthe above comparisons of the various areas one concludes that Negro Harlem is better off in some respects than Area IV, nearly 100 per cent white, let us hasten to add that the poorest Negroes are gradually moving into this area; and that when Negro families move into an area, no matter how run down, the rentals generally rise.

2. Rentals Paid for Family Quarters

The Negroes in Harlem have constantly protested against the comparatively high rentals which they are forced to pay. That these complaints are not without foundation was clearly shown in the testimony of Mr. Langdon Post before the commission. He pointed out the fact that the majority of the rentals paid by Harlem families on the lower East side were under $20. On the basis of data collected by the New York City Housing Authority it is possible to show that rentals tend to increase in proportion to the percentage of Negro families in the various areas which we have compared above. In Table VII below, we find that 57.3 per cent of the families in Area I, where Negro families comprise 90 per cent or more of the families, pay from $30 to $49.99 for family quarters, whereas in Areas II and III with increasingly smaller proportions of Negro families, 47.0 and 41.3 per cent respectively of the families pay such rentals. In Area IV, a practically white area with dwelling

TABLE VII

PERCENTAGE DISTRIBUTION OF FAMILIES ACCORDING TO MONTHLY RENTALS IN AREAS COMPRISING CENSUS TRACTS GROUPED ACCORDING TO PERCENTAGE OF NEGRO FAMILIES IN TRACTS

Monthly Rentals	Census Tracts in Which of Total Families Negro Families Comprise			
	90 Per Cent And Over Area I	76 to 89 Per Cent Area II	40 to 75 Per Cent Area III	Under 5 Per Cent Area IV
Under $1.00	0.8	1.1	1.5	4.7
$10 - $19.99	7.6	6.3	10.6	35.2
20 - 29.99	23.1	22.3	29.1	41.2
30 - 49.99	57.3	47.0	41.3	41.2
50 - 74.99	10.5	19.1	13.3	16.9
75 - 99.99	0.6	3.3	3.0	1.1
100 - 149.99	...	0.4	0.7	0.1
150 and over	...	...	0.1	0.1
Total	99.9	99.5	99.6	99.5

slightly more deteriorated on the whole than Area I, only 16.9 per cent of the families pay rentals within the same range. Although there are only about

7 per cent more dwellings in Area IV needing major repairs than in Area I, 35.2 per cent of the families in the white area pay rentals between $10 and $19.99 as compared with 7.6 per cent for Area I, the Negro Area. Moreover, in Area IV over two-fifths of the families pay between $20 and $29.99 as compared with 23.1 per cent in Area I.

Half of Income Goes to Rent

We can get a closer view of the rental situation in Harlem by studying the information which the New York Housing Authority collected last year on family incomes in six Harlem blocks. Let us view two of these blocks. First, taking the block bound by 137th and 138th streets and Seventh and Lenox Avenues, we find that 60 per cent of the 374 Negro families paid over 50 per cent of their income for rent.

The total family incomes in this block amounted to $33,723.70, of which $17,578.24 was earned by male heads of families; $5,298.66 by female heads of families; $3,951 from other members of families, and $3,872.30 from lodgers. In addition to the earned income, the 62 relief families, who constituted 16 per cent of all families, received $1,937.27, which amounted to 6 per cent of the gross total income. The average income per family in this block was $88.27, while the average rental per family was $36.69, or 41 per cent of the average monthly income.

The second block, which we have chosen from this study, showed a similar situation. In the block bounded by 133d and 134th streets and Seventh and Lenox avenues, there were 301 families, of which 122, or 42 per cent, were on relief. These 301 families occupied 21 houses, nine of which were condemned. The total incomes of these families amounted to $21,135.04, having been derived from the following sources: $10,374.80 from male heads of families; $3,473 from female heads of families; $1,118 from other family members; $1,664 from lodgers, and $4,342.24, or 20.5 per cent of the total, from relief.

The average income for these families was $70.21, of which $25.11, or 36 per cent, was spent on rentals. Ninety-seven, or about a third of the families in this block, spent 51 per cent or more of their income for rent in spite of the fact that this block is one of the worst, if not the worst, block in the Negro Harlem community.

All the figures which we have cited tend to prove that the Negro tenants of Harlem pay relatively higher rentals than tenants in other sections of the city. Moreover, they show that these high rentals require Negro families to surrender an exorbitantly large part of their meagre incomes for the privilege of living in dwellings, many of which are unsanitary and dilapidated, and some totally unfit for human habitation. That the landlords of Harlem are able to exercise such autocratic power over the lives of 200,000 people is due to the fact that Negroes cannot move about freely in the city and live where they please. The barriers which the Negro faces in his attempt to find suitable living quarters are sometimes due to the co-operative efforts of property owners.

Association Forces Negroes to Move

At the present time there is an association of property owners and residents whose purpose is to keep the Negro out of the area between 135th and 168th streets and west of Convent Avenue. Already this association has been successful in forcing Negro families to move to the east of this boundary. By thus compelling the Negro to keep within a limited territory, the landlords are able to force the Negro to pay whatever rentals they demand for their depreciated properties. Since the Negro has no choice but to live in these depreciated areas, no heed is paid to his demands for improvements. Moreover, with less money paid for maintenance costs goes more rapid depreciation, which is often charged up to ill use by the Negro families. The truth is that usually when a Negro moves into a house abandoned by whites, the house has already fallen into disrepair and, since the Negro family is in great need of living quarters, he must accept a house that is in need of repairs.

The high rents which the Negro families are forced to pay are responsible for much of the overcrowding in Harlem. The only way in which these families can meet the high rentals is by taking in lodgers. In the first of the two blocks described above, the lodgers, who constituted 17 per cent of the occupants, contributed 12 per cent of the total incomes of the 374 families; while in the second block 15 per cent of the occupants were lodgers and contributed 8 per cent of the total family incomes. In another block, included in this study, lodgers constituted 38 per cent of the occupants and contributed 34.7 per cent of the total incomes of the 75 families.

Within the limits imposed upon the free movement of the growing Negro population in Harlem, the more fortunate elements in the population have moved north and south into the houses abandoned by middle class whites, while the poorer elements have been abandoned by foreign whites after they have become unfit for human habitation. At the same time the landlord is extracting from the Negro tenant more than he could squeeze out of the white tenant. In regard to the increase in rent, the same fate has overtaken the better-situated Negro families that have sought improved living quarters in the northern section of Harlem.

Show Rent Boost To Negro Tenants

Let us take the apartment houses in the neighborhood of Broadway and 147th street, where the owners boast that they would not have Negroes in their buildings. These buildings are fireproof, provide 24-hour elevator service, and are well kept. The fairly large and light two-room apartments, provided with tiled bath, shower and dryer, and a completely enclosed kitchen unit in the living room. Such an apartment rents to whites for $37 per month.

One need only to cross Amsterdam Avenue and view similar apartments, which Negroes have succeeded in renting, to discover the power of landlords. The rentals for such apartments in similar neighborhoods usually begin at $44 and run as high as $60. The usual course of rentals in the north Harlem area, into which the better situated Negro families are attempting to find decent living quarters, is that rentals are reduced for the white tenants as a bribe to keep them in a neighborhood in which Negroes are beginning to move.

Then when the demand on the part of Negro tenants becomes voluminous enough, the white tenants are often forced out against their will, and the apartments in the houses are rented at a figure 25 to 35 per cent above that normally paid by the white tenants.

The Negro's efforts to secure decent living quarters beyond the section of Harlem in which they secured a foothold are held within bounds by the game in which the landlord is engaged to hold his white tenants as long as he can or make sure to fill his house with Negro families at exorbitant rentals. This was eminently illustrated in the case of a respectable Negro family which moved into 770 St. Nicholas Avenue.

This family was invited by the landlord to move in because he thought it was white, but when he discovered his mistake he refused the rental and finally forced the Negro family to move.

Negro political leaders were evidently afraid to come to the defense of the Negro family for fear of reprisals in an approaching election. But within two years the same landlord forced out the last remaining white families and took Negroes in at a higher rental.

Housing Protests Go Unheeded

With landlords exercising such autocratic power over the welfare and the movements of the Negroes of Harlem, it is not surprising that protests on the part of tenants against violations of the housing code go unheeded. These violations include defective fire escapes, occupancy of cellars, and faulty plumbing facilities. Often months elapse before landlords are finally ordered to give attention to these violations. Many of the landlords offer the excuse that many of the tenants are on relief or plead that their own means are inadequate to correct the evils.

In an apartment house on Seventh Avenue the seven-room apartments were rented to two or three families, or, in open violation of the multiple dwelling law which limits the number of lodgers to four, filled with lodgers. This required that thirteen to fifteen persons, including women and children, had to use one toilet. Since the majority of roomers were on relief and received a rent voucher of about $16 each, the landlord was about to make over $100 on each apartment.

These things are possible in Harlem because the people are without economic power and are thereby unable to resist the landlords who own the most necessary thing, next to food, of even physical existence. The general economic dependence of the Negro in Harlem affects the attitude of municipal authorities towards their civic rights. We have already given a description of some of the streets of Harlem, where garbage and refuse are allowed to pile up on the sidewalks. Oftimes attempts are made to excuse the filth and dirt in Negro neighborhoods on the grounds that they are due to the behavior and standards of living of Negroes themselves. However, when Negroes attempt to maintain decent neighborhoods, the attitudes of municipal authorities often nullifies their efforts. We cite the case of the block on 139th street between Seventh and Eighth Avenues, where a group of fairly well-off Negro families have undertaken to maintain the excellent physical and social character of the street.

Negroes Penalized in "Strivers' Row"

As long as white residents lived in the block, the garbage and trash were collected regularly from the rear court, but as soon as the Negro residents moved in the block they were ordered to place the garbage and trash on their front sidewalks.

It required the organized protests of the residents of this block to prevent such a manifestly discriminatory regulation in regard to Negroes. In fact, it seems that the authorities are more industrious about maintaining what they regard as the proper relations between the races than in seeing that the Negro receives his proper share of civic services. Only recently we have read in the press that a judge upheld the eviction of a white and colored woman who were living together as tenants on Lenox Avenue on the mere ground that the landlord did not want white and colored tenants to mix in his building. It seems that these tenants had with perfect right rented an apartment together and in order to circumvent the landlord's policy of charging Negro tenants higher rentals.

Our survey of the housing situation in Harlem has revealed that next to the economic problem with which it is tied up, housing constitutes the most serious problem of the community. The Negro population, increasing more than 600 per cent during the past twenty-five years, has been forced to take over the abandoned houses which were built to accomodate people on a higher economic level and with a different pattern of family life.

Instead of the Negro being free to move about and select dwelling places that suited his income and way of living, he has been forced to accept only such houses as the whites have abandoned. The landlords, profiting by the racial barriers which have restricted the movement of the Negro, have compelled him to pay exorbitant rentals and to submit to other forms of autocratic power. Consequently, the Negro being thus circumscribed has been forced in spite of high rentals to live in dilapidated and dangerous quarters without any effective means of redress. Even the municipal authorities have paid little attention to individual Negroes' complaints against the violations of the housing code, and only recently has the attention of the city been focussed on the disgraceful housing condition in Harlem.

This has been due in some measure to the organized protests which are being made by groups of tenants In their desperate economic condition the Negro tenants have ceased to accept with resignation as heretofore the exploitation of landlords and the deplorable housing conditions which segregation has forced upon them. Even if these organized protests bring about reductions in rentals and a stricter observance of the housing code, the fundamental problem will not have changed. The problem of housing in Harlem is one that will require a large scale housing program for low income groups extending over a period of years. In view of this fact, it can be readily understood that the present proposed federal housing project for five or six hundred families will scarcely touch the problem of the 56,157 Negro families in Harlem.

CHAPTER VI

THE PROBLEM OF EDUCATION AND RECREATION

Probably the greatest boon which a city like New York offers the Negro at present is an opportunity for his children to receive an education comparable to that given the white child. Since many of the children themselves received a part of their education in the schools of the South, New York City affords them their first experience in adequately equipped and manned schools. Naturally, there arise problems of adjustment which tax the patience and administrative capacity of school authorities and teachers. However, these problems are not essentially different from those arising as the result of the presence of large numbers of children of foreign-born parentage. In fact, the schools of New York City have been the one institution in which democratic principles have tended to break down racial and national differences.

Except for the West Indian element, the Negro population is native-born and the West Indians themselves are an English-speaking people. Therefore, except for the fact of color the entire Negro population--West Indian as well as the American born--would be more easily assimilated into the school system than most children of foreign-born parentage.

On the whole, Negro parents have taken advantage of the educational opportunities offered and the Negro child has become adjusted to the educational system of New York City. On the other hand, the school authorities have shown a disposition to maintain the democratic ideals of the school system by assigning Negro teachers to various sections of the city. Nevertheless, the Negro in Harlem has made serious complaints against the schools of the community on the grounds that they are old, poorly equipped and overcrowded and constitute fire hazards, in addition to the fact that, in the administration of these schools, the welfare of the children is neglected and racial discrimination is practiced.

1. Physical Aspects of the Schools

In the entire Harlem community there are 21 elementary schools, 5 junior high schools, 1 senior high school, an annex of the Straubemuller Textile High School and the Manhattan Industrial Trade School for Boys.. All of these school buildings except 4, of which 2 were leased, are brick and stone structures, the remaining being constructed of brick. According to the Annual Financial and Statistical Report of the Board of Education for 1933, 17 of these buildings are fireproof, 9 partly fireproof, and 1 of the type erected before 1892. Eleven of these buildings were erected before 1900, although 8 of them have had subsequent additions in most cases, however, before 1900. While 13 of the school buildings were constructed in 1900 or later, only 5 of these 13 have been erected since 1910. If we consider only these schools in the area in which Negroes are concentrated, we find no elementary school has been erected during the past ten years. The last school to be built in the Negro area was the junior high school at 135th Street and Edgecombe Avenue, which was erected in 1925.

In order to get a real picture of the schools which the vast majority of the Negro children attend, one must go behind the above figures concerning their age, the material of which they are constructed, and their classification relative to fire risks. One needs only to enter one of these schools to be made aware of its age which is reflected in its shabbiness, its unsanitary condition, and its antiquated architecture. Let us take a look at, perhaps, the worst of these schools, P.S. 89, at the corner of 135th Street and Lenox Avenue, which was built in 1889 and had an addition made to it in 1895. This school contains in an extreme degree all the bad features of the schools of Harlem. First of all, within a radius of two blocks of this school, there are 18 beer gardens, 6 liquor saloons, 4 moving picture houses and 2 hotels alleged to be disreputable, besides one solid block of rooming houses known to be the center of vice and the hideouts of venders of narcotics and other criminals. If one attempts to enter the building, one must be careful to step between or walk around unemployed men seated on the steps of the entrance. After entering the school building, an offensive odor greets one as he passes up the stairs leading to the principal's office and the classrooms. On the day that one of our investigators visited this building, the first thing that attracted his attention in the principal's office was a pile of old shoes strung across the floor and a pile of old clothes stacked in one corner. The principal's office was equipped with an old dilapidated desk and two chairs, one of which was broken.

Classrooms in Dilapidated State

The physical appearance of the principal's office was typical of the building as a whole. While this school has classes from the kindergarten to the sixth grade, the seats are of the type suited to kindergarten children. These seats are naturally uncomfortable for the majority of the children in the school who are over eight years of age. The classrooms are dark and stuffy; the blackboards are old and defective, and the wooden floors are dirty and offensive. At the time the visit was made to this school, 10 of the 45 rooms were out of use because of a recent fire. This school, which is classified as a partially fireproof building, has had six fires during the past four years. This school, like other schools in the Negro area, is overcrowded and therefore must run two sessions. Moreover, the school has no gymnasium or library and is generally lacking in the educational equipment which is deemed necessary in modern schools of its grade.

While this is probably the worst school in the Negro section of Harlem, the majority of the other schools show similar characteristics in varying degrees. Since most of them were built from 25 to 40 years ago, they show many of the same characteristics relative to construction, lack of equipment, and, in some cases, fire hazards. One principal excused the school's bad odor, which he tried to have overcome by spreading carbolic acid about, on the ground that students not caring to go to the lavatories outside used the stairs for toilets. In another school, where there had been a fire five years ago and the Fire Department had made recommendations, none of them had been followed. In many of the other schools, one finds the same problem of overcrowding. That this overcrowding affects chiefly the schools in which Negro children represent the majority of the pupils is shown by the figures on schools having more than one session. Of the 9 schools in this area, only 1 school with practically 100 per cent Negro attendance has a single session. In 5 of these schools in which Negro children constitute from 85 to 100 per cent of the pupils, there are three sessions in three schools and double sessions in the other two. The remaining three schools in which Negro children constitute from 10 to 20 per cent of the pupils have only single sessions. In addition to two and three sessions in at least half of the elementary schools, there are between 40 and 50 pupils per class.

2. Administration and Educational Problems

Overcorwding under any circumstances would tend to make more difficult the problem of discipline. Therefore, it is not surprising to find that in these schools discipline presents a serious problem. However, there are other factors that are responsible for the situation in regard to discipline which we find in these schools. While it is of course impossible to say to what extent each factor is responsible for the general lack of discipline in these schools, one may indicate in what way each contributes to the present condition. We shall consider, first, the teaching staff in these schools, not however because they are primarily responsible, for we believe that there are more fundamental factors. It seems that many of the white teachers appointed to the schools of Harlem regard the appointment as a sort of punishment. They look upon their appointment in Harlem in this way, not only because they are to teach Negroes, but also because of the conditions under which they teach. At any rate, there appears to be a great deal of turnover in the white personnel of these schools. It is quite natural that teachers who regard their work in this light certainly will not have a sympathetic attitude towards the children who present many behavior problems in the Harlem schools. In the second place, it appears from observation that a disproportionate number of older white teachers are to be found in the Harlem schools. It has been claimed that these teachers have asserted their right to remain in the schools in which they have served a long time, although the influx of Negroes has brought new problems, or they have been appointed to serve in Harlem until they were eligible for retirement. These older teachers are naturally impatient and unsympathetic towards the children. Moreover, the problems presented in these shcools often require the physical vigor and energy which only young men and women are able to exert. These statements in regard to white teachers in Harlem are not criticisms directed at white teachers as a group for many of them exhibit an intelligent and sympathetic understanding of Negro children which some Negro teachers in these schools do not possess.

No one should expect teachers, either white or colored, to overcome the deficiencies in training which result from broken homes, poverty, a vicious environment, retardation, and ill health. Yet the general lack of discipline which the teachers have to deal with is due in part to all of these factors. About 25 per cent of the Negro families of Harlem are broken families, i.e., families with only a woman as head. According to the principal of one of the schools of Harlem, in 699 of 1,600 families represented by the children the father was either dead or had deserted his family. That delinquency among the children seemed to be tied up with broken homes appeared in the report of another principal who found that 75 per cent of delinquent children in his school had come from broken homes. These facts covering the family background of a large percentage of the school children of Harlem are indicative of some of the social and cultural factors which must be taken into consideration in relation to the lack of discipline. They call attention to the vicious neighborhoods surrounding these schools. One principal, in denying that there was a sex problem in his school, admitted that men and older boys who did not attend the school often chased girl students into the school and attacked them.

_t is not surprising that this happens since it appears that the principals are powerless to exert any pressure on the police to prevent such occurrences or to close the vicious resorts which are allowed to operate in the neighborhood of the schools. It is difficult to say to what extent the vicious behavior exhibited by the students in their practice of carrying weapons or in their homosexual relations is a direct reflection of the vicious environment about the schools.

Poverty Among Children High

Since poverty, as we have shown in the third chapter, is the problem of primary importance to the Negro in Harlem, it is responsible for many of the problems of the schools in the community. Many of the children stay away from school because of the lack of food and especially clothing. Many come to school hungry and are listless or complain because of the lack of food. In one school alone, 1,000 free lunches were served daily. The lack of nourishment is responsible for low vitality and makes the children susceptible to disease. In a junior high school, between January 4 and June 20, 1935, there were 139 cases of malnutrition and eight cases of tuberculosis brought to the attention of the school authorities.

Along with delinquency, truancy, and ill health, retardation constitutes one of the major problems of the schools of Harlem. Like these other problems, it cannot be considered in isolation from the other social problems of the schools or the social and economic problems of the community. Overaged pupils in the classes create problems of discipline and are responsible for delinquency and truancy. Some of the retardation is due to the fact that these children received part of their education in the schools of the South.

But one cannot discount the general environment from which these children come in the City of New York. In some of the schools, 25 per cent or more of the children are retarded. While special classes to deal with this problem are found in some of the schools, on the whole, personnel and equipment are lacking.

In fact, one of the most serious charges that must be brought against the schools in Harlem is that they lack the personnel and the equipment which modern schools have at their disposal for handling intelligently and efficiently the social problems of the pupils, as distinguished from the educational problems in the traditional sense of the term. Recreational facilities are lacking in most of the schools. Children are forced to use the streets for playgrounds and thereby are thrown in contact with the vicious elements in the community. Very few schools have the services of a visiting teacher. Harlem is the only section of the city without nursery schools, although no section needs them more than this area of broken homes and with a large proportion of mothers who must work. Moreover, if a Negro child is on the verge of delinquency, the school principals do not have the assistance of psychologists and psychiatrists. Usually the child is dismissed from school without any further provision since there are no juvenile homes to which it can be sent. In regard to the health of the school children, the same situation prevails. There is no program for dealing systematically with the health problems of the children in this area. Moreover, welfare agencies co-operating with the schools have not made the same provisions for sending Negro children to camp and the seashore as they have done in the case of the whites.

3. Discriminatory Practices

Although the public schools of New York City are supposed to be free from racial discrimination and we have already commented upon the extent to which they have lived up to democratic ideals, our study of the school system in Harlem has brought out many forms of discrimination which are racial in character. First, "The grossly unfair, discriminatory and prejudiced treatment of the Negro child appears from the fact that the Board of Education in asking funds from the federal government for 168 new school buildings in New York asked for but one annex in Harlem." In spite of the conditions which we have described above, of the $120,747,000 asked only $400,000 was earmarked for schools attended by the vast majority of colored children. Although this program has been abandoned, it indicates the general attitude of the school authorities towards the educational needs of the Harlem community.

Moreover, our investigations enable us to point to types of discrimination which have become established practices in the Harlem schools so far as Negro pupils are concerned. In this connection, we turn our attention first to the Wadleigh High School where most of the Negro girls in the Harlem area are required to do their senior high school work. The main building of this school is located on 111th Street between Seventh and Eighth Avenues and has two annexes, one in 102d Street and the other on 135th Street at Convent Avenue. About 30 per cent of the student body is Negro, the remainder being divided as follows: white American and Jewish, 25 per cent each; Italian, 15 per cent, and Spanish, 5 per cent. All of these racial groups are represented on the teaching staff but for some reason the name of the Negro teacher who has been at the school three years does not appear as a member of the teaching staff in the school's handbook. Most of the Negro girls--about 75 per cent--attending this school are pursuing courses in dressmaking, domestic science and other vocational courses which are given in the main building. Only 10 per cent of the pupils in the 102d Street annex, where the commercial courses are given, are Negro. In the 135th Street annex where the academic work, preparing pupils for entrance to institutions of collegiate standing is given, only 15 per cent of the pupils are Negro. But in the special courses which prepare girls for the outstanding women's colleges not a single Negro girl was enrolled. A comparatively large number of these Negro girls, about 12 per cent, are dropped from the academic department because of deficiencies.

Inadequate Training at Junior High Schools

In seeking the cause for the concentration of Negro girls in certain types of courses, one is naturally interested to know whether it is due to their peculiar aspirations, intelligence and general social background or to some selective and directing influence exercised by the school authorities. In the first place, the relatively small number of Negro girls who go from the junior to the senior high school is due to the fact that they are selected on the basis of their attainments in the junior high schools. Many of these girls are deficient in their training, not because of any fault of their own, but because the poorly equipped and crowded junior high schools of Harlem do not give them adequate preparation for entrance to a senior high school. While this accounts in part for the small number entering the senior high school and their concentration in the vocational courses, it is not the whole story. The selection is due in the main to the policy of the educational advisers. These advisers, often reflecting the traditional belief concerning the capacity of the Negro for purely academic pursuits, direct these girls into vocational courses. But there are restrictions concerning the vocational courses. These educational advisers discourage Negro girls from taking the commercial courses on the ground that opportunities are not open to Negro girls in the commercial field.

The problem of giving vocational guidance to the Negro children of Harlem is an especially difficult one even for the fair-minded educational adviser. As one seemingly conscientious and intelligent adviser put the problem: Should she direct Negro children into lines of occupation according to their intelligence and interest, although it was known that Negroes were not employed in such occupations; or should she, taking into consideration this fact, direct them into fields in which they would be likely to find employment? While it is true that a conscientious adviser may be conscious of the problem involved, as a matter of fact, it requires more than conscientiousness. Some of these advisers have no knowledge of the occupations in which Negroes have been able to enter in spite of traditional notions and prejudices nor are they concerned with the Negro's struggle to break down the color barrier in industry. Vocational counsellors who are charged with mapping out the future careers of Negro children in Harlem should only be such persons as possess a broad knowledge and understanding of the Negro's economic problems and who are in sympathy with his aspirations. No one who is dominated by traditional beliefs concerning the Negro's capacity for intellectual culture or his proper place in society is fit to counsel him in his choice of a career.

One School Goes To Jim-Crow Resort

While it is naturally difficult to gauge the extent of racial discrimination in the schools of Harlem, there is enough authentic evidence to justify this charge on the part of the citizens of Harlem. One needs go no further than Wadleigh High School, which we have been considering. Discrimination becomes evident, especially in the social relations of the students. This has been excused on the grounds that Southern white teachers in the school object to the mingling of white and Negro children in purely social affairs. Each year the school gives a boat ride to Indian Point Lake, where there is a swimming pool. The Negro girls are barred from the swimming pool at this resort, on the grounds that the owner has a provision in the lease that Negroes are not to use the pool. It is rumored that this restriction has not been objected to on the part of the school authorities, because it offers a means of discouraging Negro girls from going on the outing. In either case, if the owner of the resort insists upon including such provision against Negroes, it is clearly the duty of the school authorities to refuse to lease his resort. Neither the racial prejudices of Southern white teachers nor the prejudice of the owner of a pleasure resort should be of greater consideration than the insult that is offered to Negro children and the consequent damage that is done to the personality of young people by making them feel that they are unfit for association with other human beings.

Other cases of racial discrimination could be cited. But more important, though less well defined, practices of the school authorities in regard to the Negro need to be considered. For example, was it a mere accident that a visitor to one of the elementary schools saw the white girls dressed in nurses' uniforms directing visitors about, while the Negro girls were dressed as waitresses and served the visiting teachers? Most of the white teachers and principals of Harlem deny that there is any racial discrimination and generally back up their statement by emphasizing the lack of overt acts of discrimination against the Negro. This is often true, for the discrimination is subtle to the extent that the Negro is ignored or regarded as non-existent. This becomes obvious when one attends the public functions of the schools. On these occasions, when the community is requested to participate in the life of the school, one would think that there were no Negroes in the world or, at least, capable of appearing as its representatives. Of course, often the Negro is not thought of simply because many of the teachers know nothing of Negroes except in the role of servants, clowns or criminals. This has furnished the basis for the contention on the part of the citizens of Harlem that courses in Negro history should be given in the schools and that the teachers in these schools should know something of the Negro's attainments in American civilization.

Vocational Education Presents Paradox

Vocational education for the Negro in Harlem deserves separate consideration. The situation in regard to this whole question presents a strange paradox. On the one hand, it is thought proper that Negro children should have industrial training, it is said that they are not prepared for such training. So, what do we find? Let us consider the Harlem annex of the Straubemuller Textile High School, which seemingly has become a dumping ground for the dull or problem children in the area from which it draws the majority of its pupils. This school has practically no equipment to carry on the work it is supposed to do. This is, of course, no fault of the principal in charge of the school. There are no facilities to give the work of the dressmaking department, in which practically all the pupils are Negro. The shop in which electricity is taught is equipped with two dynamos supplied by the instructor himself, since the Board of Education has never put any equipment in the shop. The same is true in respect to the courses in biology, chemistry and physics. Since it is obviously impossible to give courses in this annex in any way comparable to those given in the main building, it appears that students are kept here until they reach the age limit for compulsory school attendance.

At the Manhattan Trade School for Boys, where real vocational training is given, we find relatively few Negro boys getting the advantage of the training which this school offers. Although this school is located in the heart of Harlem, nearly three-fourths of the day students come from the Bronx. The majority of the students in the evening school are Negroes. The fact that relatively few Negro students attend the day classes has been blamed partly on the principals, who make the selection, and partly on the American Federation of Labor's policies in regard to the Negro in certain trades. At any rate, it appears that, if the educational authorities were serious in their avowed intentions to give the Negro child vocational training, this school in the Harlem community should be utilized for the vocational needs of the Negro. This same observation applies to the vocational needs of the Negro girls, who comprise about 14 per cent of the students in the Manhattan Industrial School for Girls. It is claimed that Negro girls do not measure up to the standards set by this school. So, here again appears the strange paradox: Negro girls should take vocational education instead of academic work, but they are not prepared to take it! Therefore, Negro girls are directed to the vocational courses given in the junior and senior high school or sent to the Harlem annex of the Textile High School. In regard to the vocational and trade schools, attention should be called to the fact that no Negro teachers are employed in them, since it appears that they must have some years of experience in addition to their educational preparation, and this experience is denied them by the unions.

This last observation brings us back to the observation which was made at the beginning of our survey of the schools in Harlem. The school situation is related to the other problems--economic, health and housing--of the Negro. Discrimination in one field has its ramifications in all other fields of Negro life. The problem of education is the same as all other problems: namely, to make the same educational provisions for the school children of Harlem as are made for children in other sections of New York City, and to see that Negro teachers are admitted to all branches of the teaching staff as other races.

CHAPTER VII

HEALTH AND HOSPITALIZATION

1. Health of the Negro in Harlem

The problem of Negro health in Harlem is bound up with the precarious economic conditions and poor housing facilities which have been discussed in preceeding chapters. In the Harlem area as in the country at large the Negro death rate is exorbitantly high in the very diseases in which lack of sanitation and medical care, and poverty are important factors. First among these diseases which ravage the Negro population is tuberculosis. In New York City between 1910 and 1921 the Negro death rate from tuberculosis declined from 961 to 272 per 100,000, while the white rate declined from 204 to 77. Thus during the twelve-year period the Negro death rate gradually decreased at the same rate as that of the whites. But from 1922 until the present the death rate for tuberculosis among Negroes has remained practically stationary, while the rate has continued to decline until it reached 49 per 100,000 in 1934. Comparing the two races for the entire twenty-five-year period ending in 1934, we find that at the beginning of the period the Negro rate was 175 per cent in excess of the white rate while at the end of the period it is nearly 400 per cent in excess of the white rate. In the Central Harlem Health District where more than two-thirds of the population is Negro, the annual average tuberculosis rate for the five-year period from 1929 to 1933 was 247, as compared with 150 for the Lower West Side and 119 for the Lower East Side.

The facts brought out in a study made by the Committee on Neighborhood Health Development of the Department of Health enable us to get a clearer view of the health situation in Harlem. In this district during the five years ending in 1933 the annual average mortality rate from tuberculosis, in the four health areas with 96.3 per cent of their population Negro, ranged from 251 to 319 per 100,000. The remaining four health areas in the district, with Negroes constituting from 23.8 to 53.7 per cent of their population, showed correspondingly lower death rates from tuberculosis. The same was true in regard to the infant death rates. In the first four health areas, in which, as we have seen, Negroes make up almost the entire population, the infant death rate ranged from 94 to 120 per 1,000 live births. Although we cannot present the rates of new cases of venereal diseases for the individual health areas, it should be noted as indicative of the general situation in the entire district with 90.1 per cent of its population composed of Negroes that the annual average venereal disease rate for the years 1929 to 1933 was 3,133 per 100,000. This was more than twice the rate for the next highest rate which was found on the Lower West Side. The Central Harlem Health District excels all other districts in Manhattan in maternal and diphtheria mortality, and in the incidence of whooping cough. Its mortality rate for all causes--14.8 per 100,000--is about the same as that of the Lower East Side which is exceeded only by the Lower West Side.

2. Harlem's Health Agencies

In the entire Harlem area, as defined in the third chapter, there are 17 volunteer hospitals, 8 proprietory hospitals, 1 municipal hospital and 1 state institution. However, in the Central Harlem Health District where the Negro population is concentrated there are 3 proprietory and 3 volunteer hospitals and the municipal hospital, Harlem Hospital. In this same district maternity hygiene and child hygiene are carried on in the Health Center and four substations, three dental clinics, and a venereal clinic for pregnant women and infants. The co-operating agencies--the New York Tuberculosis and Health Association, the Henry Street Visiting Nurses' Association, the Speedwell Society for the Care of Convalescent Children and the American Red Cross--which formed the Central before the creation of this health district have remained a part of the present organization. The Public Health Nursing Service is carried on by a staff composed of a district supervising nurse, two assistant supervisors and thirty-three staff nurses. Four physicians as well as members of the nursing staff carry on medical work in the schools. The tuberculosis service in this district is centered in Harlem Hospital which we shall consider separately.

The present organization of agencies to take care of the health of the Negro in the community has come up for criticism for two reasons: first, because the public health nursing service which is under the Civil Service of the city government represents a racially segregated unit, and second, because the facilities for taking care of the popular health problems of the community are inadequate. The entire nursing unit, including senior and junior supervisors and staff nurses, is composed of Negroes. In spite of the patently false reasons given for the concentration of Negro nurses in the district, evidence indicates that it was a deliberate attempt to establish a Jim-Crow health set-up. Miss Amelia Grant, director of nursing service of the Board of Health, claimed that this was done in the interest of efficiency after consultation with a Negro nurse, but the same Negro nurse has denied the assertion. The facts in regard to the assignment of Negro nurses in this district and the restricted authority of the Negro supervisor shows conclusively that the organization is deliberately creating a segregated unit. Negro nurses were transferred from other districts to work in this district. In one instance two Negro nurses were transferred from the Presbyterian Medical Center because it was stated that there was objection to Negro nurses in the tuberculosis clinic at the Medical Center. Two other cases show even more clearly that the policy has been to maintain the Negro character of the unit. When an attempt was made to appoint a Negro nurse in the place of a white nurse who had served for a long time at P.S. 156, which is in the district, and the school protested, the Negro nurse was placed there in spite of the protests. Racial discrimination is even more glaring in the case where the same was attempted at the All Saints' Catholic School. When objections were made to the substitution of a Negro nurse the white nurse was retained, and, in spite of the fact that she remained in the Central Harlem District, this white nurse was placed under a white supervisor in another district. The facts leave no doubts concerning the policy of segregation and justify the protests which have been made against such a policy.

Improper Supervision in Health Agencies

A superficial comparison of the health agencies in the Central Harlem District where the Negro population is concentrated and those in the East Harlem District with only about 10 per cent of its population Negro, shows no noticeable differences. But in a closer scrutiny of the two health organizations we find that in the Central Harlem District only 1.7 per cent of the time was given to tuberculosis which is the major health problem in the area. Moreover, eight physician gave their time to tuberculosis in the East Harlem District, whereas only one served this need in the Central Harlem

District. Moreover, in the latter district only 1,427 nursing visits were made to the schools while 11,471 nursing visits were made to the schools in the East Harlem District. Although the Central Harlem District had the advantage of venereal disease treatment--only for pregnent women and infants--yet only five per cent of the time of the health set-up was given to this disease which snows, as pointed out above, more than twice as high an incidence as in any other health district.

Even if we concentrate our attention only on the East Harlem District we find that the two health areas in this district where the Negroes are concentrated have been neglected in regard to health agencies. The first annual report of the Bureau of District Health Administration, Department of Health, states: "There is need for further prenatal care in Health Area 20 which is the most northerly of the six health areas served by the Rainhard Center and which is so remote that the mothers will not come to the center." It turns out that Health Area 20 is one of the two areas in which the Negro population is concentrated in the district. These facts have furnished grounds for some of the complaints which have come before the commission concerning the inadequacy of facilities in the Harlem community. But most of the complaints have been directed against Harlem Hospital, to which we shall now give our attention.

3. Harlem Hospital--Health in Community

The present problem of Negro health in the Harlem community is epitomized in the situation which has been found at the Harlem Hospital. This is true not only because it is the only municipal hospital in the area, but more precisely, because of its practices and policies in regard to Negro physicians, nurses and patients and because of the role which this institution has been forced to assume in the struggle of the Negro for equal status in New York City. For the past fifteen years Harlem Hospital has been a storm center about which the battle was first waged for admission of Negro physicians and nurses. As a result of incessant agitation, Negro doctors have been gradually placed upon the staff and Negro nurses have been admitted to training. But in spite of these changes in policy, complaints have continued concerning the training of Negro nurses. Moreover, the community has also registered its dissatisfaction with the facilities which the hospital has at its disposal for taking care of the health of the community.

The commission, therefore, set as its task a full inquiry into these various complaints as well as the larger problem of the role which the Harlem Hosptial has had to play in accommodating Negro doctors to the discriminatory practices on the part of the municipal hospitals of New York City. Let us take a look first at the physical aspects of the Harlem Hospital. Our report refers, of course, to the situation before the Women's Pavilion, which remained uncompleted for four years, was opened after we had completed our investigations. The present equipment and facilities of the hospital were designed for a much smaller task than is now placed upon it. With a bed capacity of 325, it was not an unusual occurrence for the hospital to accommodate as many as 450 patients. The Commissioner of Hospitals, Dr. Goldwater, at the hearing before the commission on November 8, 1935, admitted himself that Harlem Hospital was more overcrowded than any other hospital. As a result of this terrific overcrowding, patients were forced to give up their beds periodically; cots were placed in the hallways; couches were squeezed between beds; stretchers were used as beds; and some patients were forced to sleep on chairs. In other respects the inadequate facilities and the old and worn-out equipment of the hospital make for an unbelievable situation in a civilized community. For example, as a result of the fact that the elevator which was installed for patients has been out of order for more than a year, patients are carried up and down on the elevator which is used for garbage. It was found that the ventilating system in one of the kitchens had been out of order for over a year and that a refrigerator in one of the kitchens contained spoiled meat. The rubbish and roaches which were found in other units of the refrigerating system were characteristic of the general conditions of the kitchens which were cluttered with rubbish. In the yard of the hospital where garbage was stored, piles of rubbish furnished a happy hunting ground for scavengers in the neighborhood.

In addition to these deplorable physical conditions, there was found to be a general lack of discipline and supervision. Even to the casual observer this was visible, inasmuch as the telephone booths were hang-out places for outsiders as well as employees and the corridors were used, both night and day, as public thoroughfares by persons going from 136th street to 137th street. Within the hospital itself the lack of discipline became even more evident. The lack of discipline was even visible in the behavior or orderlies towards their superiors. They often refused to give adequate assistance to the nurses and created confusion in the set-up as they hauled rattling trucks through the corridors and noisily ordered the bewildered patients about. The lack of discipline on the part of the hospital staff has created hardships on the patients and has helped to give Harlem Hospital the bad name which it has in the community. Bus loads of patients destined for other hospitals have been parked in the hospital yard for over an hour because the intern who was in charge could not be found. Such matters as the routine transfer of patients to other hospitals, instead of proceeding smoothly under the supervision of a responsible person, were delayed for hours because of the indecision on the part of nurses and the absence of proper supervision. These instances, which could be multiplied many times, give a sufficient insight into the general lack of discipline in the hospital.

While it is obvious that the efficiency and competence of an institution cannot be judged by rumors and hearsay concerning it, nevertheless it appears that many rumors and beliefs current in the community concerning the treatment of patients at Harlem Hospital are not without foundation. It is not surprising that as a result of lack of discipline and overcrowding patients are subjected to risks and hardships which one would not find in a well managed hospital. The admittance facilities for children, which Dr. Goldwater acknowledged should be improved, require immediate correction.

For example, on one occasion, in view of twenty-five or thirty terrified and disgusted children, a bloody operation was performed by a doctor and a nurse. Another example of the little regard which is shown for the feelings and physical well-being of patients is furnished in the case of a respectable citizen when he went to the hospital for a fractured arm. According to the sworn testimony of this patient before the commission, immediately upon entrance to Harlem Hospital she was asked if her injury were due to some disreputable conduct. Then it appeared that the treatment given this patient was highly questionable, for she continued to suffer and went to another hospital where it was found that the wound had suppurated. Although it is impossible to say how widespread such cases are, they are sufficiently numerous to create rumors in the community and produce a feeling on the part of the citizens of Harlem that Negro welfare is being neglected.

Hospital Staff Lacks Morals

The lack of discipline at Harlem Hospital described above appears to be due in a large measure to the general lack of morals in the medical staff. Without going into details concerning the problem of the Negro at Harlem Hospital, it appears that the relation of the Medical Board to the hospital staff is such as to create the belief among the medical staff that the board is not a democratically controlled group as it should be, but that one white member of the board exercises autocratic authority and is sustained by the Commissioner of Hospitals. While it is inevitable that in any institution there will be politics, the present form of control and management of Harlem Hospital produces a demoralizing situation in which personal attachments and subservience to an autocratic rule outweigh meritorious services and efficiency in one's special field. We cite as a specific example the case of a doctor who had been recommended for promotion and received the approval of nine of the ten members of the Medical Board but failed to receive his promotion because of the opinion of a single member of the board, Dr. Bullowa, who was sustained by the commissioner. While this situation does not affect solely the status of the Negro members of the staff, it tends to assume a racial character when the present white dictator on the Medical Board goes so far as to remove notes and findings of a Negro physician from a patient's chart. Yet, despite the persistent charges of race prejudice against Dr. Bullowa by Negro physicians connected with the Harlem Hospital, Commissioner Goldwater dismissed them on the grounds that the accused doctor had an outstanding reputation in the medical profession and was an expert in his field. Moreover, he excused Dr. Bulbwa's refusal to appear before the Mayor's Commission on Conditions in Harlem when requested to testify on the situation at Harlem Hospital by indicating that Dr. Bullowa might have appeared had he been assured that the problems could be discussed without informing agitators and misleading the public.

The attitude of Dr. Bullowa towards the Negro doctors is of primary importance, since one of the major causes of the present unsettled condition at Harlem Hospital is the struggle of the Negro physicians for recognition. The leaders in this struggle are not men who desire to lower the standards of scientific medicine in order to give positions to Negro physicians. In fact, Negroes who have won a place in the Harlem Hospital have exhibited a high degree of efficiency and have been in favor of maintaining the highest standards of the medical profession, even if it required the dismissal of inefficient Negro doctors. Likewise, Negro doctors are not disposed to underrate Dr. Bullowa's scientific ability, but insist that his racial attitude, like that of Hitler towards the Jews, causes him to ignore and belittle the scientific ability of medical men who are black.

Goldwater Pledges Co-operation

In regard to this aspect of the situation at Harlem Hospital, Commissioner Goldwater assured the Mayor's Commission that he would be glad to probe any question involving any irregular and improper conduct on the part of an official in the hospital if it were brought to him through the regular channels. However, his assurance in this regard provides little solace in view of the difficulty which aggrieved Negro doctors experience in getting a hearing through these "regular channels," for it seems to be a matter of common knowledge that freedom of speech, when it involves criticism of the system at Harlem Hospital, is tabooed. While Dr. Goldwater declared that he is willing to assert that "so far as my official acts are concerned, since I took office January 1, 1934, no official act has been due to race prejudice or political pressure," his subsequent remark that every minority group is a victim of race prejudice and has been for all time leaves the Mayor's Commission unconvinced that he will take a positive stand against discrimination against Negro doctors. Of the same nature was his observation that "it is the most natural thing in the world for a man who belongs to a minority group that has received unfair treatment, to attribute it to prevalent prejudice." While there may be a measure of truth in these observations, it is also true that human progress cannot be achieved by taking a cavalier attitude towards such evils, but only in proportion as mankind works to break down barriers erected against men and women because of the accident of race, color, creed or nationality.

How the failure to break down discrimination against Negro physicians and nurses in the hospital set-ups in New York City has handicapped them in their competition with members of other racial groups is clearly shown in the case of Negro nurses. At the present time, Negro nurses are admitted to only four of the municipal hospitals including the Harlem Hospital. Whatever charges have been brought against their training at the Harlem Hospital must be laid at the door of the hospital authorities who insist upon treating Negroes as a separate racial group. For example, while Negro nurses are given the opportunity for graduate courses in psychiatry offered at the Bellevue Hospital, they are not permitted as are the white pupil nurses to do ward work or to live in residence at the hospital but must return to the Harlem

Hospital. Commissioner Goldwater, in testimony given before the sub-committee on hospitals of the Mayor's Commission, November 8, 1935, cited the fact of Negro nurses taking the course in psychiatry as a new opportunity which had been given them under his administration. But he was unable to explain why Negro nurses were not permitted to do ward duty and pleaded ignorance of this phase of the makeshift course which is offered Negro nurses. But it should be observed that Negro nurses are given three months of tuberculosis experience at the Sea View Hospital despite the fact that it is known that, because of overwork at the Harlem Hospital, which is inadequately manned with nurses, they are especially susceptible to tuberculosis. That their health is definitely endangered by this disease is evident from the fact that for the period, February 5, 1934, to February 4, 1935, 14.5 per cent of the pupil nurses contracted clinical pulmonary tuberculosis. Thus it appears that discrimination against the Negro nurse has gone so far that the authorities are willing to give them the regular nurses' certificate, although they have not had the prescribed courses and that they are forced to work under conditions which constantly endanger their health, even their lives.

The problem of Negro health and hospitalization in the Harlem community is bound up fundamentally with the general status of the Negro in New York City. The appointment of Negro nurses and physicians in Harlem Hospital was regarded at first as a partial victory on the part of Negro citizens in their struggle to obtain the rights and privileges of other citizens in New York City. But this so-called partial victory, instead of opening the way for the appointment of Negro physicians and internes in the municipal hospitals, is turning out to be a policy of systematic racial discrimination with all its attendant evils. From what has been stated above concerning Harlem

Hospital, it is clear that the shameful physical condition of the hospital, the lack of proper consideration for patients, the absence of morale in its administration, and its inadequate nursing staff, are all due to the failure of the hospital authorities to treat the Negro as other citizens. Racial segregation in this instance, as in all other instances where segregation is practiced, has resulted in a lower standard of efficiency and treatment for the Negro. If Negro doctors, internes and nurses were appointed to all the municipal hospitals just as members of other racial groups, and if Harlem Hospital were not made the clearing house for the transfer of patients from other institutions, then the same standards would prevail at the Harlem Hospital as at other municipal hospitals. There would be no need of makeshift courses for Negro nurses; there would be no question of racial representation on the Medical Board. Merit and attainment in the medical profession alone would determine the appointment of Negro nurses, doctors and internes. But the Negro doctor, under the present policy of segregation, is handicapped from the start in his efforts to qualify himself to compete on equal terms with other physicians. It is obvious that if the Negro physicians and surgeons are not given an opportunity to practice in the different municipal hospitals under various teachers, they can never attain the completeness of technique and experience which will qualify them to take their place beside these who have achieved distinction in the medical profession. In the matter of appointment of Negroes to the municipal hospitals, which according to law are forbidden to practice racial discrimination, the Commissioner of Hospitals need only follow the example of the retired Superintendent of Schools, Dr. O'Shea, who saw that Negro teachers were placed in schools throughout the City of New York.

What has been stated in regard to Harlem Hospital applies with equal force to the general situation in Harlem. Because of its poor housing facilities, its unsanitary conditions, and its poverty, the Harlem community is a breeding place of a high tuberculosis and infant mortality and other diseases. As long as these underlying conditions continue, the community will need adequate health agencies to deal with these diseases. But these health agencies must be set up on the same principles as agencies in other sections of the city and administered as part of the general health organization of the City of New York. Any attempt at a segregated health unit such as has been organized in the Public Hearings Service will not only perpetuate the present discrimination against the Negro but will also handicap him further in his struggle to survive in the urban environment.

CHAPTER VIII

CRIME AND THE POLICE

In view of the social and economic conditions in Harlem, described in previous chapters, one would expect to find considerable crime in that community. Hence, in analyzing the crime situation in Harlem, one must keep in mind the social and economic setting in which the crimes occur; otherwise the analysis will be valueless either as a means of understanding the casual factors involved or as a guide in establishing remedial measures. Chronic unemployment, poverty and dependency, deteriorated dwellings, inadequate health agencies and poor educational and recreational facilities all help to create a community situation in which crime thrives. Such a social environment and economic situation as one finds in Harlem begins its deadly work on the children, many of whose mothers must bear a large part of the burden of supporting their families. Even these adults who have escaped being schooled in crime under such conditions often run afoul of the law because they are deprived of an opportunity for normal economic activities. Moreover, in an environment where community control is at a minimum all sorts of wild and undisciplined impulses find expression. When the more fortunate residents realize that conditions in Harlem encourage anti-social and criminal behavior and thereby place a heavy burden upon the police, they feel, nevertheless, that the police of Harlem show too little regard for human rights and constantly violate their fundamental rights as citizens. Therefore, in this chapter we shall discuss, first, the question of juvenile delinquency; second, the problem of adult crimes; and third, the behavior and attitude of the police towards the citizens of Harlem.

1. Juvenile Delinquency On the Increase

From the proportion of Negro children arraigned in the Children's Court, it appears that juvenile delinquency among Negroes has been increasing during the past fifteen years. The proportion of Negro children arrrigned in the Children's Court increased from 4.2 in 1919 to 11.7 in 1930. Yet, from the figures in the following table on the number of Negro boys and girls arrested in Harlem for juvenile delinquency for the years 1930 to 1934, inclusive, it appears that the number of Negro boys arrested for juvenile delinquency has increased during these five years in spite of the slightly upward trend in the last two years.

TABLE VIII

NUMBER OF NEGRO BOYS AND GIRLS ARRESTED FOR JUVENILE DELINQUENCY AND NEGLECT IN SEVEN POLICE PRECINCTS IN THE HARLEM AREA FROM 1930 TO 1934, INCLUSIVE.

	Total Homes in the Harlem Area									
	Total Persons Under 16 Arrested		Juvenile Delinquency				Neglected			
			Ages 10 - 16		Ages Under 10		Ages 10-16		Ages Under 10	
Year	M	F	M	F	M	F	M	F	M	F
1930	425	43	339	25	37	0	5	7	8	5
1931	302	25	245	14	18	1	7	2	7	5
1932	231	32	193	17	.8	0	3	1	4	9
1933	230	38	210	26	9	1	2	1	7	4
1934	295	45	233	26	8	0	6	1	8	7
Total ...	1503	183	1240	108	80	2	23	12	34	30

(Continued on Page 108)

TABLE VIII (continued)

Homes Outside Harlem Area,
Address Unknown
No Homes

	Juvenile Delinquency 16 Years and Under Male, Female	Neglected 16 Years and Under Male, Female
1930	24	18
1931	21	7
1932	23	5
1933	21	7
1934	30	1
Total	119	38

In considering this table the first fact that impresses one is the large number of neglected and homeless children who come to the attention of the police. During the five years, 137 boys and girls were arrested because of neglect, ten of whom had no homes. It will also be observed that most of the neglected children are under ten years of age. This reflects no doubt the breakdown of family life which figures so conspicuously in the social disorganization of this area. The same cause is apparent in the case of the relatively large number--32 for the five years--of children under ten years of age arrested for juvenile delinquency.

In Table IX above, where the charges against these delinquent boys are given, we find that about 25 per cent of them were arrested for larceny, robbery and stealing, and about 10 per cent for burglary and unlawful entry. Thus it appears that more than a third of those boys were arrested upon serious crimes involving property. On the other hand, it appears that the delinquency of an equally large number was due to activities that could be

TABLE IX

OFFENSES CHARGED AGAINST BOYS AND GIRLS ARRESTED IN THE HARLEM AREA FROM 1930 TO 1934, INCLUSIVE

Charge	Total Persons Arrested		Homes in Harlem Area				No Home Address Unknown Homes Outside H. A.			
			Ages				Ages			
			10 - 16		Under 10		10-16		Under 10	
	M	F	M	F	M	F	M	F	M	F
Larceny										
Robbery, Stealing ...	386	7	359	6	12	0	15	1	0	0
Incorrigible way-ward minor	69	65	60	30	0	0	23	12	0	1
Burglary										
Unlawful entry	158	2	143	2	4	0	11	0	0	0
	19	38	14	33	2	3	3	3	0	0
Hold-up	42	0	37	0	0	3	2	0	0	0
Malicious mischief ..	104	5	91	5	3	0	5	0	0	0
Assaults	58	6	54	6	1	0	3	0	0	0
Auto theft	20	0	19	0	0	0	1	0	12	0
Neglected	83	54	23	12	34	30	14	0	0	0
Hitching on trolleys	134	0	153	0	0	0	1	6	0	0
Stealing subway rides	188	0	153	0	8	0	24	0	0	0
Miscellaneous	276	14	235	6	12	0	0	1	1	0
Total	1547	163	1304	120	115	52	114	24	13	7
Persons charged with more than one of-fense	44	0	0	2	2	0	1	0	0	0
Total persons ..	1603	163	1203	120	114	32	113	24	13	7

controlled through proper recreational agencies in the community. For example, about 20 per cent of the boys were arrested for hitching on trolleys and stealing rides on the subway. Moreover, attention should be called to the offenses--270 in all--classified as miscellaneous. While this classification includes three cases of homicide, the vast majority of juvenile arrests under the miscellaneous classification in Table IX were due to such offenses as selling newspapers after 7 o'clock in the evening and shining shoes on the streets. Certainly, these latter offenses are bound up with the generally low economic status of the families in the community, and like adult delinquency can only be understood in their social setting. Therefore, one may conclude that juvenile delinquency in Harlem is due primarily to the lack of adequate recreational facilities and to social disorganization resulting chiefly from the poverty of the community.

2. Adult Delinquency Caused by Poverty

Just as juvenile delinquency thrives in an environment of poverty, broken homes, lack of recreational facilities, and vice, adult delinquency has its roots in the widespread social disorganization of the Harlem community. According to the records of the seven police precincts in the Harlem area, during the first six months of 1936, there were 6,348 Negro men and 1,336 Negro women arrested. A little more than seven per cent of the men and about five per cent of the women were under 21 years of age. On the other hand, the majority of the men--59.1 per cent--were between 31 and 35 years of age, while over two-thirds--67.6 per cent--of the women were between 21 and 30 years.

The causes of these arrests are very revealing. Among the men, policy, or what is known as the numbers racket, stands first, with 2,089 or 31.0 per cent of the total arrests. It is important to note that men arrested on this charge are numerous in all age groups to sixty. One hundred and fifty men arrested on this charge were between fifty and sixty. This will occasion surprise to those acquainted with the operations of this illegal lottery in Harlem. The widespread operations of this racket, which extracts so much money from the community for the benefit of racketeers who have no other interest in Harlem are due to a large extent to the desperate economic conditions of the people who hope to gain through luck what is denied them through labor.

Although policy figures less prominently among the causes for women's arrest, it accounts for 8.5 per cent. The next major cause for arrests among Negro men showed almost the same proportion as policy; this is disorderly conduct, which included 2,023 arrests, or 30.9 per cent. This term included many types of misdemeanors, a great many of which were immoral conduct. In fact, most of the 255 arrests of women--practically a fifth of the women arrested--were due to immoral conduct.

However, the majority of women arrested--801 or 59.9 per cent--were charged with vagrancy, another term often used to designate immoral conduct. Three-fourths of these women were between 21 and 30 years of age. Thus it appears that close to 80 per cent of the Negro women arrested in Harlem were arrested on charges due to immoral sex behavior. In an environment like Harlem, where there is little opportunity for employment for the large number of single women who have broken away from the family ties, immoral conduct offers a means of livelihood.

Five crimes involving property--burglary, 188 arrests; robbery, 141 arrests; grand larceny, 77 arrests; assault and robbery, 32 arrests, and pickpocketing, 24 arrests--together accounted for 7 per cent of the arrests of men and 3 per cent of the arrests of women. The next three crimes of importance as causes of the arrests of men were gambling, felonious assaults, and liquor violations. The 421 arrests for gambling constituted 6.4 per cent of the total; while the 334 arrests for violations of liquor laws amounted to 5.1

per cent of all arrests. It is especially important to note the figures in regard to crimes against persons since social and economic conditions in Harlem are conducive to such crimes. Of the 6,540 men arrests, 328, or 5.0 per cent, were charged with felonious assaults, and 35, or five-tenths of 1 per cent, with homicide; while of the 1,338 women arrested, 38, or 2.8 per cent, were charged with felonious assault and 4, or three-tenths of 1 per cent, with homicide.

Negro Criminals Are Disorganized

In considering the above figures in regard to the crime situation in Harlem, several facts should be borne in mind. Negro criminals are not organized, and thereby do not offer the same threat to life and property as organized gangs. On the whole, Negro crimes result from the fact that normal individual impulses and desires are often forced to express themselves in a lawless manner in a disorganized social environment. In connection with the above statistics, it should be observed, first, that 281, or 4.3 per cent of the men, and 67, or 5 per cent of the women arrested, actually resided outside of Harlem; and secondly, that the arrests of white persons have not been included in our summation.

The main purpose here has been simply to present figures on the extent to which Negroes in Harlem were arrested and to indicate the major crimes with which they have been charged. Those figures cannot be regarded as an index of the criminality of the Negro; since, aside from economic and social factors, involved in Negro crime, those figures reflect the attitudes and arbitrary practices, as we shall see, of the police of Harlem.

A final consideration must also be kept in mind in regard to criminal behavior in Harlem. Primarily because of its poverty, the people of Harlem can exercise little control in the economy of the city. Therefore, Harlem becomes the prey of every influence that is capable of wielding economic power in the community. It has become the location of vice dens and pleasure resorts for whites.

White people come to Harlem in order to escape the control of their own communities. In Harlem they indulge in vicious and anti-social behavior because they are free from the censure of their race and their intimate groups in which their lives are rooted. The Negro, because of his helpless economic condition, must cater to the vicious, immoral and pleasure-seeking impulses and desires of these whites. Hence, as long as Harlem remains an area in which whites, and Negroes, for that matter, can throw off normal social restraints, it will remain a breeding ground for crime and delinquency.

3. The Police in Harlem

Nothing revealed more strikingly the deep-seated resentments of the citizens of Harlem against exploitation and racial discrimination than their attitude toward the police when the latter were called to testify before the commission. This resentment was not due solely to killings that had dramatized the brutal behavior of the police. It was due in a large measure to such incidents as that related in the following letter to the mayor.

"West ---th Street
N.Y.C. April 26, 1935.

"Mayor Fiorello LaGuardia,
City Hall, N.Y.C.
"Your Honor:

"I wish to respectfully call your attention to a very high-handed act of the police of the Twenty-third precinct.

"My wife and I occupy one room and kitchenette at the above address.

"On Tuesday morning, April 16, 1935, between 10 and 11 o'clock, the superintendent of the house rapped at my door. Upon opening it, I was confronted by three men (men in civilian clothes) who the superintendent said were policemen. He explained that the men were searching the house, for what he did not know.

"The men entered the room, and proceeded to search without showing shields or search warrant. I asked twice of two of the men what was the reason for such action. I received no answer from any of them.

"My dresser drawers were thoroughly gone into, dresser cover even being raised. My bed came in for similar search, covers were dragged off and mattress overturned. Suitcase under my bed was brought up and searched. My overcoat hanging on the door was gone over and into. My china closet was opened and glassware examined. After this startling act the man left my room, still without saying a word.

"Now, Mr. Mayor, we are a law-abiding, honest, Christian couple, having never run afoul of law and order. This police action has caused us quite a little worry, especially as there is no assurance that it will not happen again.

"We have brought this incident to your attention, feeling that you will have the matter looked into, and that you will advise us as to our next step in the matter.

Respectfully yours,

-------------------"

One might be inclined to believe that the incident was false, or at least exaggerated, had not policemen themselves testified at the hearings that they entered the homes of Negro citizens without a warrant and searched them at will. The case of Herbert Patterson, a Negro, which was heard before the commission offers an excellent example of the behavior of the police in Harlem.

Condemn Entry Without Warrant

"The records of the Police Department show that on May 5 an anonymous telephone call was received stating that this man was wanted in Philadelphia on the charge of murder and that he had concealed weapons in his house. Several hours later two detectives entered Patterson's home without a warrant, routed him out of bed, searched for concealed weapons, found none and brought him to the police station.

"Patterson stated that he had come from Philadelphia, that he had known the man he was accused of murdering, that the deceased had died in Harlem Hospital in New York and that he had been released after an earlier inquiry into the same matter. Still the police did not release him but communicated with the Philadelphia police who then asked for his fingerprints. After they were received in Philadelphia, the police there declared that Patterson was not wanted as there was no record of any such murder. After two days in jail, Patterson was released."

Thus it appears that the police arrested an innocent man on an anonymous complaint, in spite of the fact that the law requires that a citizen be not arrested, when charged with felony, without a warrant or unless the arresting officer has definite knowledge that a felony has been committed and reasonable cause to believe that the person charged or suspected committed the felony. In this case the police went beyond the law in arresting Patterson and searching his home, for the detectives had neither the warrant nor the knowledge required by the statute. The commission asked Inspector Di Martini, Lieutenant Battle and the detective who made the arrest for their interpretation of the law. It was not in accord with the statute and the commission felt that the large audience was justified in shouting that the law is not being applied in connection with arrests of Negroes.

The insecurity of the individual in Harlem against police aggression is one of the most potent causes for the existing hostility to authority. One of the excuses which the police offer for illegal searches of persons and their property is the quest for policy slips. We have already shown above that 2,000, or 31.9 per cent of the arrests in Harlem during the first six months of 1935 were for this offense.

After a witness had testified before the commission that his home had been subjected to illegal search for policy slips, more than twenty-five indicated in response to a question by the commission that they had had similar experiences, only one admitting that he had had policy slips in his possession. Another occasion that often affords the police of Harlem an excuse for invading the personal rights of its citizens is when white and colored people are seen consorting together.

Although the police are especially likely to interfere if a colored man is with a white woman, one witness testified before the commission that he was arrested and taken to the police station because he was walking with a colored woman. He was held for a time until he could prove to the officer that he was a colored man. Moreover, it was brought out by white witnesses, who were arrested during the riot, that the police attempted to impress upon them by words and acts of brutality that whites were not to associate with "the black bastards in Harlem."

In the chapter on the outbreak of March 19, reference has already been made to the inexcusable killing of Lloyd Hobbs and the attempt of the police to justify the killing by not only making the boy appear as a burglar escaping with his loot, but also by changing the record in the police station. Another instance of police brutality, which occurred just six days prior to the outbreak of March 19 and aroused considerable resentment against the police of Harlem, was the Aikens case.

"Thomas Aikens, a young Negro, 28 years of age, and who came from a respectable family, was standing in a breadline in the 369th Infantry Armory Building on March 13, 1935. He had gone to the Armory in order to get a free meal because, being unemployed, he did not want to depend entirely upon his relatives and friends.

"When Mr. Aikens got in line, at about 10:30 in the morning, there were about 150 men ahead of him. At about 1:30 in the afternoon, when the line had reached the point where he would have soon received his food, he was shoved a bit out of line by other men, who had placed themselves in line. At this point, two policemen, namely, David Egan and Eugene Cahil, came to him and, with abusive language, told him to go to the end of the line, which now had increased to about 500 men. Aikens protested, stating that he was out of line due to the constant pushing by the men and that he had a right to remain where he was, having been in line since 10:30 in the morning.

"With this protest, he was labeled a 'smart nigger' and immediately was set upon by the two police officers, who were assisted by another white man, known as 'Cap,' who is in charge of feeding the men who come to the Armory. Aikens was first struck in the mouth by a blunt instrument and, as a means of protecting his face, he threw up his hands. Someone from the rear struck him on the head and again he was struck in the face and in the left eye.

"At this point he fell to the floor unconscious, and he lay there nearly thirty minutes. Finally he was dragged across the Armory floor and the policemen put in a call for the patrol wagon. However, someone else had called for an ambulance from Harlem Hospital, which responded before the patrol wagon. Aikens states that he could hear the policemen telling the ambulance surgeon to clean the blood from the face in order that he could be taken to the police station.

"The doctor is reported to have stated that the man (Aikens) was in a serious condition, which necessitated his being taken to Harlem Hospital, where he was admitted as a prisoner and received emergency treatment. The admitting physician diagnosed the injuries as being 'traunstic rupture of the left eyeball.'"

When the arresting officer became aware of the serious results of his brutality he created a defense for his actions by charging Aikens "with willfully and wrongfully striking an officer on the left side of face with clenched fist." Aijens was conned as prisoner at Harlem Hospital, where an operation was performed to save his injured eye. On March 20, when the physicians thought his condition had improved sufficiently to permit him to be moved, he was transferred to the prison ward of Bellevue Hospital. There another attempt was made to save his eye, which finally had to be taken out.

"On April 10, Aikens was discharged to the Twelfth District Court, where he was arraigned before a magistrate on a charge of felonious assault preferred by the arresting officer, and the bail was set at $600, which was later reduced to $25, and the case was adjourned until April 23. The case was adjourned on several occasions after the above date by request of the arresting officer, who was represented by Assistant District Attorney Leo, assisted by the officer's personal counsel. At another hearing before Magistrate Kress, sitting in the Seventh District Court, it was found that the corroboration of the officer's testimony made a prima facie case and, with no other alternative, the judge sent the case to the grand jury."

Patrolmen Rehearse Their Answers

On April 20, the subcommittee on crime of the commission convened to hear testimony regarding the Aikens case. After Mr. Aikens testified, the chairman of the subcommittee asked Patrolman David Egan if he wished to testify. He replied by stating, "I do not with to testify. Whatever testimony I would give would defeat the ends of justice." Patrolman Eugene Cahil was asked if he wanted to testify. He replied by repeating, word for word, the statement made by his fellow officer. It was obvious that the two patrolmen had rehearsed their answers, although it was doubtful whether they could have told what was meant by their statements. These officers were backed in their refusal to testify by a letter from the District Attorney, William C. Dodge, addressed to the Police Commissioner.

When we consider the part which the medical superintendent of Harlem Hospital played in the defense of the brutality of the policemen in the Aikens case it will help to show why the residents of Harlem have so little faith in that institution. Since Patrolman Egan had claimed in court that he had suffered a laceration of the mouth and several of his teeth had been knocked out, a diligent search of the records of Harlem Hospital was made. No record was found of a policeman's having been treated. Finally, the medical superintendent admitted that he had given the policeman involved a statement to the effect that he had been treated at the hospital. Thus it is apparent that an official in one of the most important institutions in Harlem is willing to assist policemen in their efforts to justify their brutality towards Negroes.

Another case of alleged brutality, occurring a few days after the outbreak of March 19, was brought to the attention of the Commission. This case involved Patrolman Labutinaki who, in August, 1934, had shot and killed a 16 year old Puerto Rican boy because he ran, after being surprised in an act of burglary. In the case of immediate interest, Patrolman Labutinaki was called about four o'clock on the morning of March 25, 1935, to arrest one Edward Laurie, a Negro, 32 years of age, who was charged with disorderly conduct by a Negro manager of a restaurant on Lenox Avenue. Evidence was presented to show that Laurie had been drinking and that he struck the policeman a slight blow.

Patrolman Labutinaki struck him in return with such violence as to knock Laurie to the sidewalk, fracturing his skull so badly that he died in the hospital fifty minutes later. Even if the story of the officer is accepted as entirely true, it is obvious that he was in no jeopardy whatever, and that Laurie was unsteady on his feet and was totally unarmed. Here, then, was a case in which good police work, such as pinning the man's arm and leading him away, would have prevented a killing and thereby not offered further confirmation of the belief of the majority of the Negro citizens of Harlem that the life of a Negro is cheap in the estimation of the police.

The cases which have been cited here indicate to what extent the police of Harlem invade the rights of Negro citizens.

This invasion of the rights of Negro citizens involves interference in the association of whites and Negroes, searching of homes without a warrant and the detention of innocent men in jail, and even the mutilation and killing of persons upon slight provocation. Of course, in fairness to the police it should be stated that there are many conscientious and humane policemen, who are not guilty of these offenses against the citizens of Harlem.

Yet, inasmuch as the Police Department makes no effort to discipline policemen guilty of these offenses, but either hides behind such subterfuges as the exoneration given by grand juries or actually justifies the infringement of the rights of Harlem's citizens, then the Police Department as a whole must accept the onus of these charges. For example, in response to a letter from the chairman of the subcommittee on crime and the police of the Mayor's Commission setting forth these complaints against the police of Harlem, the police commissioner, Lewis J. Valentine, maintained that there was no reason for disciplinary action against the police, stated the action of the grand jury without comment in each of the cases, and even justified the action of the police in the Patterson case.

Such attempts on the part of the police officials to justify the brutality and aggression of the police only encourages disrespect for authority in general and antagonism towards the police as representatives of law. The citizens of Harlem understand that the invasion of their rights and the slight regard that is shown for their lives is due not only to the fact that they are Negroes, but also to the fact that they are poor and propertyless and therefore defenseless.

When one of the policemen was asked if he would have acted towards the citizens on Fifth Avenue and Park Avenue as he had acted towards those in Harlem, he hesitated, stammered, and finally gave no answer. But in spite of the helplessness which their poverty imposes upon them, the citizens of Harlem are realizing more and more the power of their organized number. The outbreak of March 19, though spontaneous and without leadership, is strengthening the belief that the solution of their problems lies in mass action. Police aggressions and brutalities more than any other factor weld the people together for mass action against those responsible for their ills.

This naturally creates a dangerous situation in Harlem in that an act of brutality or aggression on the part of the police may at any time act as a spark and set off an explosion which will have more serious consequences than the outbreak of March 19. Therefore, it is clearly the responsibility of the police to act is such a way as to win the confidence of the citizens of Harlem and to prove themselves the guardians of the rights and safety of the community rather than its enemies and oppressors.

CHAPTER IX

CONCLUSIONS AND RECOMMENDATIONS OF COMMISSION

On March 19, 1935, several thousands of Harlem's citizens, after five years of the depression, which had made them feel more keenly than ever the injustices of discrimination in employment, the aggressions of the police, and the racial segregation, rioted against these intolerable conditions. This spontaneous outbreak, the immediate cause of which was a mere rumor concerning the mistreatment of a Negro boy, was symptomatic of pent-up feelings of resentment and insecurity.

Today, extra police stand guard on the corners and mounted patrolmen ride through the streets of Harlem. To the citizens of Harlem they symbolize the answer of the city authorities to their protest of March 19th. To Harlem this show of force simply signifies that property will be protected at any cost; but it offers no assurance that the legitimate demands of the citizens of the community for work and decent living conditions will be heeded. Hence, this show of force only tends to make the conditions which were responsible for the occurence last March 19th more irritating. And so long as these conditions persist, no one knows when they will lead to a recurrence, with possibly greater violence, of the happenings of that night.

The commission wishes therefore to present its conclusions relative to the data on these conditions presented in the preceding chapters and to offer such recommendations as seem proper to deal with them in order to allay much of the present unrest in Harlem.

The first and most fundamental problem of the Negro citizens of Harlem is the economic problem. While it is true that the present economic crisis has been responsible for the appalling amount of unemployment and dependency in Harlem, the great mass of the workers in the community live even during normal times close to the subsistence level and many of them are forced to be supported by charitable agencies. The majority of Negro men are employed as unskilled workers and in domestic and personal service, while 85 per cent of the women are engaged exclusively in the latter type of occupation. The generally low economic status of Negro workers is, of course, due fundamentally to the operation of our competitive capitalistic system. Negro workers, being newcomers to the city and the most recent entrants into industry, are on the whole marginal workers.

But, in addition to the operation of the factors which are inherent in our economic system, there are certain social factors which keep the Negro worker in the ranks of unskilled laborers and in a state of perpetual dependency. The main social factor which is responsible for this condition is racial discrimination in employment. It is this factor more than any other factor that arouses so much resentment in the Negro worker. If the economic system through competition, he reasons, inevitably condemns many workers to a starvation level, then he demands the right to compete on equal terms with other workers for a decent standard of living. This, he is not permitted to do.

Racial discrimination as a factor in limiting the employment of Negroes is especially characteristic of the public utilities. These corporations upon which the community must depend for such necessities as heat, light, and the means of communication and transportation have maintained a strict color caste in regard to employment. Thus the Negro is forced by necessity to give up a relatively large part of his meager earnings while these corporations remain adamant in the policy of excluding Negroes from employment.

However, they are teaching the Negro slowly but surely the lesson that only through collective or public ownership of the public utilities can he enforce his right to employment on the same basis as other races. While the Independent Subway System attempted in the beginning to apply the caste principle to the employment of Negroes and allowed them to work only as porters, when this system was placed under civil service, Negroes were able to assert their legal right to compete on the same basis as other people. While the Negro worker has only won a more or less paper victory, he has placed the City of New York in a position where it must either uphold the laws or follow the example of private employers in keeping the Negro in menial positions at starvation wages.

Our analysis of the policy of discrimination in the employment of Negroes as practiced by private employers has been set forth above. Here we need only emphasize the fact that when employers exclude Negroes from employment or place the badge of inferior status upon them by keeping them in menial positions, they are only helping to make more acute the conflict between the employers and a large section of an urban proletariat which is coming to look more and more upon employers as mere exploiters. When the outbreak occurred last March, the black proletariat attacked property, which had become a symbol of racial discrimination and exploitation without even the compensating virtue of offering means of employment.

However, we are fully aware that private employers count upon competition between white and black workers as a means of holding the unemployed and dependent black masses in check. The attitudes of many unions confirm this faith, since, as we have shown above, they are among the chief obstacles to the employment of Negro workers. Yet these very craft unions, by their exclusion of Negro workers, are driving them into the camp of labor leaders, who see that the craft organizations are ineffective as a means of securing the rights of labor. More specifically, labor unions that discriminate against black labor cannot expect to be recognized as the representatives of labor.

The Negro worker gets a certain revenge against a community that discriminates against him through the money which the community must spend upon him in the form of relief. Discrimination against the Negro in employment is responsible at all times for a large number of Negroes who are supported by the relief agencies. The present economic crisis has simply accentuated the dependency of the Negro. But in the relief setup, as in other institutions in the community, Negro personnel was not employed upon the basis of individual merit but according to the prevailing conceptions concerning the Negro's proper place or status in relation to whites. For anyone to argue that Negroes were given positions in the personnel of the Home Relief Bureau solely on the basis of individual merit exposes him to the charge of being unbelievably naive or dishonest. To be sure, racial discrimination was not as open and brutal as in private employment, but it accomplished the same end.

For example, Negroes were not put in such strategic positions as to see that work relief was given on an equitable basis. While naturally many mistakes were made in the classification of relief clients, mistakes do not explain the fact that most Negroes, no matter what their skill, were given the classification of laborers. It was only the standardization of relief budgets that prevented many Southern-born white relief workers from giving Negro families a smaller allowance which would have conformed to their ideas of the needs of Negroes. At any rate, it appears that only in the giving of home relief was the Negro treated on the whole as other citizens.

In view of the Negro's impoverished condition, it is not surprising to find him living in the often dilapidated and dangerous living quarters which whites have abandoned. Innumerable housing conferences, after having discussed the deplorable housing conditions of the Negro, have either passed resolutions or made known their desire that the Negro should have more wholesome housing. But nothing has resulted from these pious and sentimental expressions of humanitarian feelings. No doubt it is true, that, to give a new context to an old saw, if wishes were houses Negroes would live in palaces.

But houses are built for people who can pay a price that assures a profit to the contractor. Since building contractors do not find it profitable to construct homes for the low income groups among the whites, it is not surprising that Negro wage earners who live on the margin of subsistence cannot find decent homes. But here again color caste places an additional burden upon the Negro tenant. Crowded in a black ghetto, the Negro tenant is forced to pay exorbitant rentals because he cannot escape. He is the veritable slave of the landlord, and because of the helplessness which his poverty and ignorance imposes upon him, he cannot force municipal authorities to see that he gets the minimum protection which the housing laws provide.

We must turn again to the economic factor for an explanation of the ravages of tuberculosis and infant mortality in the Harlem community.

Ignorant and unsophisticated peasant people without experience with urban living would naturally find survival difficult in the city; but when poverty and inadequate health agencies are added to their burdens, they are doomed to extinction! Thus we find in Harlem that the Negro's battle against tuberculosis seemingly was bringing victory until, following the migrations from the South, the death rate ceased its downward trend about fifteen years ago. The health agencies, as in the case of housing, were designed for a community with a different pattern of life and a different set of problems. There has been no systematic and comprehensive effort to modify these agencies to serve the needs of the present community.

Harlem Hospital, the chief health agency in the community, has taken on Negro physicians and offered training to Negro internes and nurses; but this has really been one with the apparent intention of transforming the hospital into a Jim Crow institution. The lack of morale among the medical staff, the treatment accorded the patients, and the general management of the hospital have all indicated that standards are being set up to harmonize with the generally inferior status of the Negro as a distinct racial group.

As with the health agencies, so with the educational institutions which the Negro inherited when he took over a community which the whites had abandoned. The disgraceful physical condition of the schools of Harlem as well as the lack of recreational facilities and the vicious environments that surround the schools, all indicate the presence of a poverty-stricken and therefore helpless group of people in the community. One can almost trace the limits of the Negro community through the character of the school buildings.

That these conditions are due primarily to the fact that the Negro community is powerless to force the indifferent city authorities to afford adequate educational and recreational facilities was forcibly demonstrated by the fact that a recently proposed building program involving the expenditure of $120,747,000 included only $400,000 for an annex in Harlem, although most of the schools in this area were built before 1900.

Such an environment as Harlem is naturally a breeding place of juvenile and adult delinquency. What has been found in Harlem concerning juvenile delinquency only confirms the studies that have shown the decisive influence of community disorganization as a complex of causative factors no matter what racial group inhabits such a community. Yet in the case of Harlem we find few of the agencies that have an ameliorative influence upon juvenile delinquency. In regard to adult delinquency, we find no organized criminal gangs, but a preponderance of such crimes as flourish among poverty-stricken and disorganized people. Moreover, the fact should be stressed that the very economic impotence of the community and its subjection to exploitation by outside interests, such as the policy racket and the location of institutions in the community for the pleasures and vices of whites, who seek this means of escape from the censure of their own groups, encourage anti-social behavior and nullifies the efforts of responsible citizens to maintain social control.

While one would not expect the policemen in Harlem to show any appreciation or understanding of the sociological factors responsible for crime in the community, the discipline of the Police Department should see to it that they do not become the persecutors and oppressors of the citizens of the community. Nevertheless, it is true that the police practice aggressions and brutalities upon the Harlem citizens not only because they are Negroes but because they are poor and therefore defenseless. But these attacks by the police upon the security of the homes and the persons of the citizens are doing more than anything else to create a disrespect for authority and to bring about mass resistance to the injustices suffered by the community.

The commission fully realizes that the economic and social ills of Harlem, which are deeply rooted in the very nature of our economic and social system, cannot be cured by any administration under our present political and civic institutions. Yet the commission is convinced that, if the administrative machinery set itself to prevent racial discrimination in such municipal institutions as the schools and the city's subway system and penalized, as far as possible, private concerns and individuals that practiced racial discrimination, the people of Harlem would at least not feel that their economic and social ills were forms of racial persecution. Therefore, the commission makes the following recommendations.

First, in regard to discrimination in employment, the Commission recommends:

1. That the city enact an ordinance to the effect that no contracts may be given to any firm or labor union that discriminates against Negro workers.

2. That the city make some provision in its contract with the public utilities concerning the employment of Negro workers.

3. That the Negro consumers of Harlem present an organized protest to the public utilities concerning the discrimination against Negro workers.

4. That since the present wages of the porters in the Independent Subway System are not sufficient to guarantee a decent standard of living, the wages of these employees be increased to the maximum allowed under Civil Service Regulations.

5. That Negroes be permitted without police interference to carry on peaceful picketing of establishments refusing to employ Negro workers on the same terms as white workers.

6. That officials in the Independent Subway who attempt a discrimination against Negro workers be dismissed from their positions.

7. That Negro workers organize and cooperate with white workers in breaking down racial barriers in the labor unions.

Second, in respect to the relief situation, the Commission recommends:

1. That a committee of white and colored persons representing Harlem consult with the present head of the Home Relief Bureau with a view to clearing up the questions concerning the status of Negro personnel in the Bureau. We consider this action necessary since, while the present executive has attempted to correct some of the injustices in the Bureau, the confidence of the Harlem community in the Bureau can only be restored by some sort of cooperation and understanding between representatives from Harlem and the Bureau.

2. That a Negro be appointed without salary to see that the present discriminations in work relief be given publicity and those responsible be dismissed.

Third, in regard to housing, the Commission recommends:

1. That the New York City Housing Authority be empowered to plan for a period of years a housing program for Harlem.

2. That the authorities of the City of New York enforce the housing code and condemn the dwellings unfit for habitation.

3. That the tenants of Harlem organize and protest against exorbitant rents, and if such protests are ineffectual, that they refuse to pay rentals until some equitable agreements are reached.

Fourth, in respect to ecucation and recreation, the Commission recommends:

1. That P.S. 89 be condemned and torn down and a modern school building be erected on the site or on a more suitable site which the city may choose.

2. That the necessary funds for the immediate launching of an emergency building program in Harlem be asked for and obtained from Washington.

3. That additional school quarters be secured forthwith--there are some idle buildings reported immediately available--in order that classes be reduced

with all possible speed.

4. That every effort be made to secure additional playgrounds in cooperation with the churches, the park authorities and welfare agencies; that the huge armory of the 367th Infantry be hired for properly supervised play and games; that funds be secured to keep all existing school playgrounds open under adequate control until 6 p.m. in term time, and all day long in the vacation period; that unemployed teachers also be utilized for conducting groups of children to the more remote parks for supervised recreation. Since it appears that relief funds have been spent for much less important things, we respectfully urge immediate filling of this far more important human need.

5. That the staff of teachers and especially of visiting teachers be increased as fast as possible.

6. That the present system of letting the cleaning of the schools to custodians for a lump sum be abandoned since it leads to politics, often to inadequate cleaning, and to the underpayment of the personnel employed for this purpose.

7. That the Board of Education be asked to devote itself particularly to the Harlem problem in the interest of the public safety and order.

8. That a conference be called at once of representatives of those agencies dealing with children, and especially delinquent, deficient or backward children, to see if the needs of the similar Negro children cannot at least in some temporary degree be met forthwith.

9. That a Negro be appointed to the Board of Education whenever this becomes possible.

Fifth, in respect to health and hospitalization, the Commission recommends:

1. That colored doctors and nurses be admitted to all municipal hospitals

in accordance with the law which prohibits racial discrimination in tax supported hospitals.

2. That the number of colored doctors on the medical staff of the Harlem Hospital be increased; it being understood that their appointment will be based upon merit.

3. That a new hospital of equal size as the present Harlem Hospital be built or that the present hospital be enlarged to twice its present capacity, because we of the commission are convinced that while there is the possibility of such overcrowding all the evils cited in this report must of necessity continue. It is also the opinion of the commission that some arrangement should be made whereby Harlem Hospital be relieved of the duty of acting as a clearing house for the transfer of patients from other institutions. This, we believe, would help to relieve the conditions of congestion and apparent confusion.

4. That the number of nurses in the training school at Harlem Hospital be brought up to the quota demanded by nursing standards. This is absolutely necessary because of the shocking development of tuberculosis among the pupil nurses due to the overcrowding and overwork with its attendant fatigue and lowering of resistance to disease.

5. That Negro nurses of Harlem Hospital be given the identical provisions for affiliated training on contagious diseases and psychiatry that exist for all other nurses in training. The commission at the present time is cognizant of a plan to offer Harlem nurses lecture courses in place of the regular affiliate course which requires residence. In regard to the assignment of colored doctors and nurses in the Department of Hospitals, the commission would call to

your attention the contrast in attitude of the present commissioner of hospitals and the stand of the Board of Education when Dr. O'Shea, retired superintendent of schools, stated publicly that there was no such thing as a Negro teacher in the New York City school system. Dr. O'Shea's justification for this stand is seen in the assignment of teachers of Negro extraction to schools in all parts of the city regardless of the racial status of the pupils.

6. Since morale is almost completely broken down among the staff of the Harlem Hospital, a complete reorganization of the Hospital, including the medical staff and the Medical Board seems to be the only adequate means of assuring the efficient functioning of this institution.

Sixth, in respect to crime and the police, the Commission recommends:

1. That the police in Harlem be instructed--and the violations of these instructions be backed up with disciplinary measures--that it is not their business to interfere with the association of whites and Negroes. It should be impressed upon them that their private prejudices are no warrant for such interference and that such interference will lead to dismissal from the police force.

2. That the police in Harlem close up the dives and pleasure dens that cater to the vices and disreputable pleasures of white patrons. It is especially urged that any cabaret, dance hall or any other form of institution for entertainment in Harlem that refuses to admit Negroes and thereby advertises itself as such a place be closed by the police.

3. That the commissioner of police arrange for the appointment of a committee of from five to seven Harlem citizens of both races to whom colored people may make complaint if mistreated by the police. The commissioner properly points out that he can do little to better conditions if complaints are not

made to the Department. But to this the reply is that the citizens are fearful of making complaints lest there be unpleasant consequences to them and they thereby gain the ill will of the police. It is contended also that complaints are ordinarily referred back to the precinct where the incident arose and there pigeon-holed. We feel sure that the situation would be greatly improved if there were a body of citizens to sift all complaints and to take up with the commissioner, personally, if necessary, such cases as merit attention. We suggest that this committee might well also be an advisory committee, so that the head of the police may know exactly how his men are regarded by the citizens and what can be done to improve relations between citizens and their police guardians. The members of this committee should include in their number one or more men who are dissenters from established institutions and also men who are likely to have contact with victims of injustice. Obviously the committee should be quite free of either political or police domination.

4. That officers of the law who violate the law should not only be subject to investigation and punishment by the Police Department, but that action should be taken by the district attorney, where it is warranted, just as vigorously as where any other person is charged with a crime. It is too readily assumed that an officer who kills or gravely injures a citizen is acting in the line of duty and must be upheld at any cost lest the authority of the police and their power be weakened. We recommend that in every case of a shooting by the police a most careful investigation should be personally made by one of the highest officials in the department and the result of that investigation be communicated to the entire force, whether the result of the inquiry be censure or commendation. In either case the efficiency of the force would be improved.

5. That a system be devised by which, in the event of any further happening likely to cause grave public disorder, the Police Department would be in a position to set forth the truth by distributing leaflets and placards besides giving the public authoritative information from high officials in the department as soon as possible. We have no doubt that radio stations owned by private interests would be glad to help in an emergency, in addition to the use of the city radio station, WNYC.

APPENDIX

CAPTIONS OF PHOTOGRAPHS APPEARING IN PUBLISHED ACCOUNT

First Photograph

"Dr. Charles H. Roberts, prominent Harlem dentist, was and is chairman of the Mayor's Commission on Conditions in Harlem, whose completed report the Mayor has not chosen to make public, but which The Amsterdam News prints for the first time."

Second Photograph

"Mayor LaGuardia has spent a good part of his recent speaking moments in Harlem denying charges made in the report of his commission which investigated conditions in Harlem. Here he is shown just about to address the general conference of the A. M. E. Church in May, at which time he essayed to answer charges of discrimination against Negro doctors by saying that Harlem Hospital has been reorganized, and that anyone who claims discrimination should be willing to submit to an operation performed by one of the surgeons allegedly discriminated against. In the picture, left, is Hubert T. Delany, tax commissioner and member of the commission, who had just introduced the Mayor, and, center, John R. Hawkins, financial secretary of the A. M. E. connection."

Third Photograph

"Attorney Eunice Hunton Carter, now of the Dewey racket investigation, was the only woman member of the Mayor's Commission, and was its secretary."

Fourth Photograph

"Dr. E. Franklin Frazier, professor of sociology at Howard University, who directed the studies and surveys which were used as a basis for the report of the Mayor's Commission. He is reported to have had a large hand in the wording of the completed report."